Visual and Performing Arts Framework

for California Public Schools:
Kindergarten Through Grade Twelve

Adopted by the
California State Board of Education

Prepared by the
Visual and Performing Arts Curriculum Framework
and Criteria Committee

Under the direction of the
California State Board of Education
Curriculum Development and Supplemental
Materials Commission

CALIFORNIA STATE DEPARTMENT OF EDUCATION • SACRAMENTO, 1989
Bill Honig, Superintendent of Public Instruction

Publishing Information

The framework, which was developed by the Curriculum Framework and Criteria Committee (see pages xiii-xiv), was edited by Janet Lundin, Theodore Smith, and Edward T. O'Malley and was prepared for photo-offset production by the staff of the Bureau of Publications, California State Department of Education. The artwork was prepared by Paul Lee and Cheryl Shawver McDonald. Typesetting was done by Anna Boyd and Lea Shimabukuro.

The framework was published by the California State Department of Education, 721 Capitol Mall, Sacramento, California (mailing address: P.O. Box 944272, Sacramento, CA 94244-2720). It was printed by the Office of State Printing and distributed under the provisions of the Library Distribution Act, and *Government Code* Section 11096.

ISBN 0-8011-0805-5

Copies of this publication are available for $6 per copy, plus sales tax for California residents, from Publications Sales, California State Department of Education, P.O. Box 271, Sacramento, CA 95802-0271.

A list of other publications that are available from the Department may be found on page 166 of this publication, or a complete list may be obtained by writing to the address given above or by calling the Sales Unit in the Bureau of Publications: (916) 445-1260.

Photo Credits

We gratefully acknowledge the use in this publication of the photographs provided by the following: Otto Greule, Young Imaginations, San Rafael, pp. viii, 6, 147; Craig Schwartz, Music Center Education Division, Los Angeles, p. x; Getty Center for Education in the Arts, Los Angeles, pp. 4, 114, 123; Carol Wheeler, Media Services, California State Department of Education, p. 6; Phil Amrhein, San Juan Unified School District, p. 7; Jack E. Howard, Sacramento City Unified School District, p. 7; Performing Tree, Los Angeles, pp. 11, 25, 56, 59; Lawrence Manning, Performing Tree, Los Angeles, p. 12; Joseph Gatto, Los Angeles County High School for the Arts, pp. 29, 67, 87, 93, 94, 108, 126; Brian Katcher, p. 36; Valerie Moseley, Performing Tree, Los Angeles, pp. 38, 60, 63, 73, 90, 140, 145, 148, 158; Bill O'Sullivan, p. 57; John C. Deichman, Jr., Music Center Education Division, Los Angeles, p. 68; Glenn Jay, San Mateo, p. 85; Patty Taylor, Visual and Performing Arts Unit, California State Department of Education, p. 111; and Bob Ware, Getty Center for Education in the Arts, Los Angeles, p. 155.

Dance

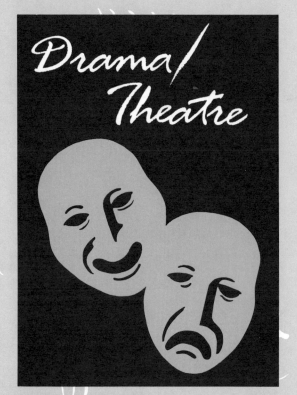

Drama/
Theatre

Music

allegro

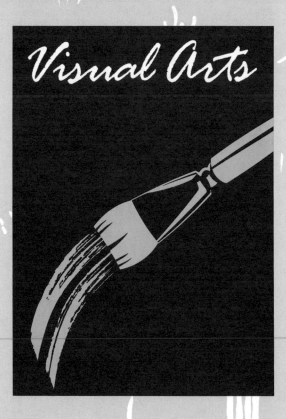

Visual Arts

Contents

Message from the State Board of Education

The California State Board of Education continues to support the aims of the *Visual and Performing Arts Framework for California Public Schools: Kindergarten Through Grade Twelve* (1982 edition). This document provides a foundation for comprehensive curriculum and instruction in dance, drama/theatre, music, and the visual arts. It illustrates what teachers and students can experience and achieve in the four arts disciplines and represents a general agreement on the goals of arts education among teachers, curriculum specialists, administrators, faculty in institutions of higher education, researchers, and members of arts foundations and professional organizations. With the reprinting of this document, there begins a curriculum and instruction cycle of assessment, planning, implementation, and evaluation that will continue until 1995.

We explore our world in many ways, through the sciences and through the arts, none of which is complete or sufficient. All are concerned with the quest for truth and the deep-rooted need to come to terms with and understand the mysteries of the world. The components for curriculum development presented in this framework reflect enlightened teaching in the arts, introducing children to many avenues for expressing what they observe, feel, and believe.

As children progress toward adulthood, they need to have an education that takes every aspect of their humanity into account. Educators have, in recent years, been increasingly concerned with identifying those aspects and establishing a core for every child's education. The arts and what they contribute are an integral part of that core; they are ways of seeing, feeling, thinking, and being.

Each of the arts provides a language for the communication of ideas and emotions. Understanding the language enables one to appreciate what others are saying; being fluent in that language enables one to say things of value to others. Those responsible for curriculum development and improvement must clearly and directly communicate to all administrators, teachers, students, parents, and the community that each of the visual and performing arts is an essential ingredient in the balanced and complete education of all students from kindergarten through grade twelve.

Some school districts and schools throughout California have already exhibited leadership in using this framework as a foundation for developing exemplary programs in the arts or have begun a long-range plan for districtwide implementation. We pay tribute to their efforts and hope they will flourish and prosper. Districts that are assessing existing arts programs and districts that are planning a visual and performing arts curriculum will find this framework essential to providing farsighted and multifaceted arts education for all students.

To support curriculum, the State Board of Education is required by the state constitution to adopt textbooks for students in kindergarten through grade eight. This framework presents criteria for evaluating instructional materials in music and the visual arts for those grade levels. Publishers should include all four components of arts education in instructional materials: aesthetic perception, creative expression, arts heritage, and aesthetic valuing. They must move beyond the traditional student-teacher text format to incorporate a wealth of instructional materials, media, and technology for instruction in a comprehensive arts program.

We extend our appreciation to those who worked in the past to develop this forward-looking framework, to those who have already implemented exemplary arts programs, and to those who continue as advocates for the arts in education. We express our thanks to the Curriculum Development and Supplemental Materials Commission, especially the Visual and Performing Arts Subject Matter Subcommittee and the State Department of Education staff, for their roles in supporting this document.

FRANCIS LAUFENBERG, President
JIM C. ROBINSON, Vice-President
JOSEPH D. CARRABINO
AGNES CHAN
PERRY DYKE
GLORIA S. HOM

MARYELA MARTINEZ
MARION McDOWELL
KENNETH L. PETERS
DAVID T. ROMERO
ARMEN SARAFIAN

Foreword

Since the awakening of humankind, artists throughout the world have expressed their ideas, emotions, and beliefs and have recorded historical events through the visual and performing arts, such as painting, sculpture, architecture, dance, movement, music, dramatics, theatre, and ceremonies. John Ruskin observed that "great nations write their autobiographies in three manuscripts: the book of their deeds, the book of their words, and the book of their art. Not one of these books can be understood unless we read the two others; but of the three, the only trustworthy one is the last." Learning through the arts makes both the book of our deeds and the book of our words come to life and reach us at a more profound and personal level. The arts are a powerful vehicle for communicating ideas and the ideals we hold to be important in a democracy.

The California State Department of Education emphasizes the visual and performing arts as significant and indispensable elements in the core curriculum. The *Visual and Performing Arts Framework for California Public Schools: Kindergarten Through Grade Twelve* represents this strong commitment to include dance, drama/theatre, music, and the visual arts in the educational life of all students as they progress from kindergarten through high school.

Two approaches to teaching dance, drama/theatre, music, and the visual arts are interwoven in a comprehensive whole in the framework. The first approach views arts instruction as direct student involvement in the expressive modes of the arts. In expressing the creative power of their minds through the arts, students become cognizant of and value their own capacities and personal uniqueness and appreciate and become sensitive to the creative expression of others. The arts are an avenue toward elevated self-concept and the acceptance of alternatives and are essential for our pluralistic school population.

The second approach to teaching views the arts as a means of acquiring cultural literacy. Students study aesthetics, cultural heritage, and the history of the visual and performing arts, including the continuing impact of the arts on all societies worldwide. Comprehending works of art at a deep and significant level of understanding helps students see these works as part of the body of knowledge defining every culture. They become aware that the arts cut across cultural boundaries to provide mutual understanding, appreciation, and respect.

The *Visual and Performing Arts Framework* is constructed on these two complementary approaches, which are expressed in four components of arts education: aesthetic perception, creative expression, arts heritage, and aesthetic valuing. The inclusion of each component in all arts instruction will allow students to become aesthetically responsive, literate, and creative citizens with a life-long interest and involvement in the arts.

Support for the arts in our schools continues to grow. Numerous national reports and articles on the status and importance of arts education have been

published, and national surveys have identified positive public attitudes toward teaching the arts in our schools.

Foundations and the business community have joined and given impetus to the growing support for the arts in education. Our own statewide plan for arts education, a joint effort with the Getty Center for Education in the Arts, provides ten major recommendations to strengthen arts education, including the provision of an articulated and sequenced arts curriculum in every school district. The unanimous conclusion is that the arts are essential in the education of our children. The stage is set, the cue has been given, and it is time for the arts to play center stage.

Bill Honig

Superintendent of Public Instruction

Preface

Since the publication of the *Visual and Performing Arts Framework* in 1982, notable developments have taken place that support and improve instruction in the arts at all levels. Dance, drama/theatre, music, and the visual arts have been established as part of the core curriculum provided at all grade levels (*Education Code* sections 51210 and 51220). The reprinting of the *Visual and Performing Arts Framework for California Public Schools: Kindergarten Through Grade Twelve* marks the beginning of a focused seven-year curriculum and instruction cycle of assessment, planning, implementation, and evaluation to improve the arts curriculum and teaching methods.

A statewide plan for arts education, "Strengthening the Arts in California Schools: A Design for the Future," recommends steps to be taken by the state, offices of county superintendents of schools, school districts, schools, and the community to advance the arts in the total curriculum at all grade levels. The California Arts Council and the State Assembly (Speaker's Task Force) have published reports on the role of arts in education. Additionally, legislation and requirements have provided wider student access to the arts. A high school graduation requirement for a year of visual or performing arts or foreign language was legislated in 1983. As a result there has been an increase in student enrollment in arts courses at the high school level. Arts courses are now accepted for entry into the University of California system, and an arts course is required for entrance into the California State University system.

Other documents support the arts framework. As required under major reform legislation (Senate Bill 813/1983), *Model Curriculum Standards: Grades Nine Through Twelve* was published by the State Department of Education (1985). Also aligned with the framework is the "Statement of Preparation in the Visual and Performing Arts Expected of Entering Freshmen." This proposed document will describe the competencies in the arts to be achieved by all students prior to entering the University of California, the California State University, or a California community college. The proposed "Visual and Performing Arts Model Curriculum Guide: Kindergarten Through Grade Eight" will also help implement the arts curriculum in elementary schools and middle schools. Information on the use of computers, instructional videos, and other technology in arts programs is presented in the Department of Education's 1987 edition of *Technology in the Curriculum: Visual and Performing Arts* (resource guide and diskette).

Drawing from the philosophical and pragmatic foundations presented in the framework and supporting documents, administrators, curriculum planners, and teachers are expected to provide a comprehensive arts education program for all students as they progress from kindergarten through high school. As a result of a districtwide assessment of how the current curriculum matches the goals established in the framework, the adoption of a formal school board policy and a multiple-year plan for the arts is recommended. The plan includes establishing curriculum goals; building support; identifying, allocating, and using resources; implementing programs for students; and providing staff development for administrators and teachers.

The assessment process may begin with an examination of the visual and performing arts sections of the State Department of Education's program quality review documents for elementary schools, middle schools, and high schools. The criteria align with this framework, and an effective program is described. During assessment, thought is given to effective programs designed to enhance every student's abilities, including students with special needs, students achieving on target, the college-bound, and gifted and talented students. The appropriateness and effectiveness of instructional resources are also considered.

The framework presents criteria for evaluating visual arts and music materials submitted for adoption. Instructional materials for each arts discipline and for the integration of the arts in other subjects should be selected. The assessment team should also evaluate the adequacy of facilities and materials, the allocation of time for the arts in the curriculum, the need for staff development, and the use of community resources in the arts program.

The personnel resources include well-informed principals who promote the arts in education, credentialed arts instructors, and trained classroom teachers. Creative investigation of assistance from other spheres results in a variety of resources enriching to the program provided by the district and school. Financial resources include national, state, or local funding and grants for specific student needs or special programs or projects. Arts agencies, outside arts providers, institutions of higher educa-

tion, museums, performing arts groups, and visiting artists or residency programs are essential resources. Parents, senior citizens, service organizations, and the business community may offer both human and financial resources and provide the advocacy essential for a quality arts program. National and state professional education associations provide members with advocacy statements, and their conferences and publications provide information, awareness, and insights related to exemplary programs.

Another facet in planning and implementing arts education is a district and school staff development design that is ongoing and is supported by the administration. This approach will ensure that those responsible for delivering arts curriculum understand the unique qualities and content of dance, drama/theatre, music, and the visual arts at a level appropriate to their area of responsibility. Integrating the arts with each other and in the other basic curriculum areas is part of the staff development design. Understanding the works of art and aesthetic values of world cultures, with special attention given to the various ethnic groups that make up the school community, is also an essential ingredient.

We wish to acknowledge curriculum commission members Ann Chlebicki, Yvonne Johnson, Joyce King, and Elena Wong, who encouraged the reprinting of this framework to achieve excellence in arts education for all students. Through a creative, inclusive, and well-articulated program for the visual and performing arts, we hope that today's students, the transmitters of culture to future generations, will understand and value deeply the role of the arts in the life of the individual and in the collective life of American culture.

JAMES R. SMITH
Deputy Superintendent
Curriculum and
  Instructional Leadership

FRANCIE ALEXANDER
Associate Superintendent; and Director,
Curriculum, Instruction,
  and Assessment Division

TOMAS LOPEZ
Administrator, Office of
  Humanities Curriculum Services

DIANE L. BROOKS
Administrator, History-Social Science
  and Visual and Performing Arts Unit

Acknowledgments

Curriculum Framework and Criteria Committee Members

Curriculum Framework and Criteria Committee

Dorothy Wilson, California State University, Chico; Committee Chairperson

Donald P. Buhman, Mt. Diablo Unified School District, Concord; Committee Vice-chairperson

Dance

Jo Ness, Glendale High School; Committee Chairperson

Conni Adams Blackwell, Cajon Valley Union Elementary School District, El Cajon

Jan Day, California State University, Los Angeles

Eleanor C. Lauer, Mills College, Oakland

Sachiye Nakano, Los Angeles Harbor College

Juan Valenzuela, Stanford University

Adele R. Wenig, California State University, Hayward

Melinda Williams, University of California, Los Angeles

Drama/Theatre

Dorothy Mulvihill, Manteca High School, Committee Chairperson

Eras Cochran, San Juan Unified School District, Sacramento

Wayne D. Cook, Performing Tree, Inc., Los Angeles

Mary Jane Evans, California State University, Northridge

Lynn Goodwin, San Ramon Valley High School, Danville

Clayton Liggett, San Dieguito Union High School, Leucadia

Sallie Mitchell, California State University, Fullerton

G. Robert Stockmann, Palo Alto City Unified School District

Music

Rosemarie Cook, Office of the Los Angeles County Superintendent of Schools; Committee Chairperson

William D. Burke, Mt. Diablo Unified School District, Concord

Joseph Curatilo, Dixie Elementary School District, San Rafael

Robert Henderson, San Diego City Unified School District

Colleen Hicks, Bolinas-Stinson Union Elementary School District, Bolinas

Cheryl Ho, California State University, Sacramento

Nancy Watling, Grace M. Davis High School, Modesto

Dorothy Wilson, California State University, Chico

Visual Arts

Kirk B. deFord, Petaluma Joint Union High School District; Committee Chairperson

Kay Alexander, Palo Alto City Unified School District

Donald P. Buhman, Mt. Diablo Unified School District, Concord

Barbara A. Connelly, Wildwood Elementary School, Piedmont

Anna W. Eng, Jordan Middle School, Palo Alto

Frances D. Hine, Office of the Los Angeles County Superintendent of Schools

Bernice B. Loughran, California Polytechnic State University, San Luis Obispo

Juana Kay Wagner, Office of the Fresno County Superintendent of Schools

Interdisciplinary Education Involving the Arts

Kay Alexander, Palo Alto City Unified School District; Committee Chairperson

Conni Adams Blackwell, Cajon Valley Union Elementary School District, El Cajon

Eras Cochran, San Juan Unified School District, Sacramento

Rosemarie Cook, Office of the Los Angeles County Superintendent of Schools

Wayne D. Cook, Performing Tree, Inc., Los Angeles

Joseph Curatilo, Dixie Elementary School District, San Rafael

Kirk B. deFord, Petaluma Joint Union High School District

Frances D. Hine, Office of the Los Angeles County Superintendent of Schools

Cheryl Ho, California State University, Sacramento

Bernice B. Loughran, California Polytechnic State University, San Luis Obispo

Dorothy Mulvihill, Manteca High School

Sachiye Nakano, Los Angeles Harbor College

Nancy Watling, Grace M. Davis High School, Modesto

Dorothy Wilson, California State University, Chico

Department of Education Staff

Francie Alexander, Associate Superintendent; and Director, Curriculum, Instruction, and Assessment Division

Diane Brooks, Manager, History–Social Science and Visual and Performing Arts Unit

Richard Contreras, Consultant, Child Development Division

Miguel Muto, Consultant, Visual and Performing Arts Unit

Lou Nash, Consultant, Arts, Instructional Services (retired)

Patty Taylor, Consultant, History–Social Science and Visual and Performing Arts Unit

Kirsten Vanderberg, Consultant, Curriculum Frameworks and Instructional Materials (retired)

Arts and Humanities Committee of the Curriculum Development and Supplemental/Materials Commission

Laurel Feigenbaum, Chairperson, 1979-80

Ruth Knier, Chairperson, 1980-81

Lucy Quinby, 1980-81

John Sanford, 1980-81

Hal Wingard, 1979-80

Introduction

During the late twentieth century, the burgeoning of arts advocacy and arts support has been unprecedented in the history of the United States. Government at all levels, private foundations, community organizations, and educational systems increasingly acknowledge the importance of the arts as a humanizing influence in a technological society.

Historically, California has been in the national forefront in developing curriculum documents for the arts; after California's curriculum frameworks in drama/theatre, music, and the visual arts were published, comparable documents were developed in a number of other states. Real improvement in education in the arts has been slow in coming, however, because of priorities imposed by fiscal problems.

An analysis of the curriculum frameworks issued by the state of California up to 1977 revealed that "each framework becomes a forecast for new educational concepts and processes within a particular discipline, while it simultaneously contributes to a vision of new educational values and goals common to all subject matter areas."[1] This *Visual and Performing Arts Framework* is an innovative document. Because it will be used in a period of rapid change, the writers have been conscious of the need to have the contents serve a dual purpose: (1) to serve as a catalyst for change based on an assessment of trends for the future; and (2) to be relevant to the current needs in education. The framework identifies commonalities among the four disciplines—dance, drama/theatre, music, and the visual arts; addresses the unique aspects of each discipline; interrelates the arts; and further relates them to the other curriculum areas.

---

[1]Ruth Knier, "An Analysis of Common Principles in Subject Matter Frameworks in the State of California." San Francisco: California Curriculum Correlating Council, 1977, p. 1.

1

The charge for this framework represented a departure from that of previous California frameworks. For the first time, four disciplines are united in one document. It is fitting that the arts should be chosen to provide a model for integrating areas of the curriculum, because they are, and always have been, a means of unifying a broad array of human experience

The Role of the Arts

Dance, drama/theatre, music, and the visual arts are disciplines with aesthetic, perceptual, creative, and intellectual dimensions. They foster students' abilities to create, experience, analyze, and reorganize, thereby encouraging intuitive and emotional as well as verbal responses. The arts provide a balance in the curriculum that is particularly important for the development of the whole person. They assist students in realizing their full potential by providing avenues for self-discovery and for harmonizing of the mind, body, and spirit, thus leading toward an integrated personality. The arts broaden expressive capacity by increasing avenues of nonverbal expression and contribute to the total learning process in numerous ways.

For all students, study of the arts can increase self-discipline and motivation, contribute to a positive self-image, provide an acceptable outlet for emotions, and help to develop creative and intuitive thinking processes not always inherent in other academic pursuits. In addition, for students who learn most effectively through nonverbal modes, the arts provide additional opportunities for successful learning experiences. Moreover, the arts can create a meaningful context for learning and can foster improved learning retention through multisensory approaches. The study of the arts can also contribute to the appreciation of historical and multicultural understandings and the development of problem-solving ability.

Schools that provide integrated arts activities as well as subject-centered arts instruction for all students can help them cultivate a positive attitude toward learning and toward coming to school—an attitude that carries over to the entire learning program.[2]

Developments and Trends

An explosion of knowledge regarding brain function as it relates to the learning process has occurred within the past decade. This, in turn, has led to new directions for curriculum planning, as educators recognize the need for developing the intuitive and creative thought processes and the importance of integrating all thought processes in the educational experience. The interrelationship of mind, body, spirit, and emotions in increasing mental and physical health as well as learning is now appreciated. Educators recognize that adequate sensorimotor development is essential to language development. For this reason, multisensory approaches to learning are particularly important in early childhood. In recent years this concept has become even more essential as the number of children entering school suffering from the lack of perceptual development is increasing.

The brain of a child differs significantly from that of an adult until the child is approximately nine or ten years of age; and, therefore, learning patterns differ, so that instruction must be adjusted accordingly.[3] Preferential modes of learning differ also according to a child's cultural background and experience. Further, since no two

[2]*Arts Impact: A Curriculum for Change.* Washington, D.C.: Office of Education, U.S. Department of Health, Education, and Welfare, 1973, p. 19.

[3]Maya Pines, *The Brain Changers.* New York: Harcourt Brace Jovanovich, 1973, p. 150.

brains are alike and because an individual's experiences also differ, each child is unique and has a unique learning pattern that needs to be accommodated.

This expanding knowledge of the individual, as well as increasing evidence of the ways societal changes affect each person, underscores the importance of the arts in education. They contribute importantly to integrating the learning process; they develop multisensory avenues of perception; they enhance the development of vital, fully functioning individuals; and their unique properties promote both individual as well as group development.

Framework Premises

The *Visual and Performing Arts Framework* reflects an awareness of trends in education and society and a growing consciousness of the need for the arts in American culture. This framework addresses this need by providing direction for restoring balance in the curriculum through the infusion of the arts and their humanizing aspects in the total curriculum. It focuses on developing important avenues of perception (visual, aural, tactile, kinesthetic) as well as positive emotional and aesthetic responses. It is intended to be a forward-looking document that will provide new directions for developing a dynamic curriculum for the schools of California.

The framework is based on the premise that fundamental relationships exist among dance, drama/theatre, music, and the visual arts and other areas of the curriculum. This premise implies a number of corollaries:

- The arts are important in the education of all students to provide for balanced learning and to develop the full potential of their minds.
- The arts provide the sensory and perceptual input essential to the

development of nonverbal and verbal communication.
- The arts can be used to vitalize and clarify concepts and skills in all curriculum areas.
- The arts can be a vital part of special education.
- The arts in general education provide an avenue for the identification of gifted and talented students whose special abilities may otherwise go unrecognized.
- The arts provide avenues for accomplishment, media for nonverbal expression, and opportunities for verbally limited or bilingual students to learn the English language.

Throughout the framework, the following terms will be assumed to have these meanings:

The arts—Encompass the disciplines of dance, drama/theatre, music, and visual art.

Aesthetic—Relates to beauty, its character, conditions, and conformity to a set of governing principles.

Aesthetic experience—Includes experience that is valued intrinsically. Whether an aesthetic experience be listening, looking, performing, or producing, involvement in such an experience carries "the desire to sustain and feel the full impact of the moment for its own sake. In an aesthetic experience one perceives the . . . interrelationships between the form and content of the experience. Such perception is what makes aesthetic experience different from other extrinsically valued experiences in everday life."[4]

---

[4]Manuel Barken, Laura H. Chapman, and Evan J. Kern, *Guidelines: Curriculum Development for Aesthetic Education*. St. Louis: CEMREL, Inc., 1970, p. 7.

Framework Organization

This framework is organized to assist curriculum planners in designing for all of the arts a curriculum that has a triple thrust—one that:

- Develops the unique characteristics of each of the arts
- Interrelates the arts
- Infuses the arts into the general curriculum as appropriate

Chapter 1 addresses the commonalities among the arts; chapters 2 through 5 present the unique aspects of each discipline. The individual discipline sections follow similar formats to assist teachers and curriculum developers in building a balanced curriculum that includes all four areas of the arts. Chapter 6 provides a guide for interrelating the arts and for integrating the arts in the total learning process. The concluding chapter articulates what is needed to develop an adequate program for all of the arts.

Chapter 1

Commonalities in Arts Education

The various arts disciplines share some fundamental components and universal goals and are described here as commonalities. These common components and goals can be used in developing an arts education curriculum.

Instructional Components

Aesthetic perception, creative expression, arts heritage, and aesthetic valuing are fundamental components of all instruction in the arts. In this framework, the goals, objectives, and teaching activities for each of the disciplines are organized under these components.

Aesthetic Perception

Each art is unique and essential in the curriculum because of the particular avenues of perception that it develops.

Increased perception sensitizes the individual to the world. As one develops a fuller awareness of the nuances of light, color, sound, movement, and composition through experiences in the arts, otherwise ordinary experiences take on an aesthetic dimension. Heightened perception provides a stimulus for imagination and creativity, and it also has an impact on all learning. In the arts, the development of aesthetic perception enables one to comprehend and respond to the elements of an object or event and to express and appreciate it in greater depth.

Creative Expression

Expression in the arts includes originating, creating and performing, and interpreting. Direct personal involvement in these expressive modes is necessary for one to understand and appreciate each discipline. Purposeful arts activities focus, channel, and encourage communication and originality, and provide increasing understanding of the structure and language of the arts. Creative expression in the arts helps one to know one's self and to appreciate one's own and others' uniqueness. Activities that lead to discovering interrelationships among the arts generate excitement, encourage creative exploration, and enhance learning.

Arts Heritage

The study of the arts within cultural contexts develops a broad base for students to understand creative artists, their works, their evolution, and their effects on society in the past and present. Knowledge of the artistic accomplishments of the great cultures of the world enables students to see the place of the arts in relation to those cultures and to grasp the relevance of the arts in contemporary society. In addition, knowledge of the arts of various cultures, past and present, helps students gain appreciation and understanding of these cultures and of their heritage.

Aesthetic Valuing

Life is enriched as the awareness and response to beauty in all of its forms increase. To develop aesthetic values, the student studies the sensory, intellectual, emotional, and philosophic bases for understanding the arts and for making judgments about their form, content, technique, and purpose. Through study and direct experience, the student develops criteria for arriving at personal judgments.

Goals in Arts Education

The overall purpose of providing educational programs in the visual and performing arts is to produce aesthetically responsive citizens with life-long interest and involvement in the arts. The specific goals for the student in any arts education program are to develop:

- Expanded avenues for communication and self-expression
- A capacity to enjoy aesthetic expression in diverse forms and to feel comfortable participating in all of the arts
- Respect for originality in one's own creative expression and sensitivity and responsiveness to the expression of others
- Skills and craftsmanship for effective expression in the arts
- Ability to use the arts to synthesize one's feelings about objective facts

- Aesthetic sensitivity
- Appreciation for the contribution the arts have made in this and other cultures, both past and present
- Intellectual bases for making and justifying aesthetic judgments based on an understanding of the nature, structure, and meaning of the arts
- Appreciation of the role of creativity in human achievement
- The capacity to experience aesthetic qualities in the environment
- Special talents and interests in the arts and occupational skills in the arts and arts-related fields

Developmental Level Charts

Each chapter in this framework contains, under the heading "Developmental Level Charts," a section which includes several pages of charts. These charts are organized, first, by the four components discussed above. The goals and objectives that contribute to each of these components are listed at the top of each chart, and areas of content, whether organized by subject matter or by process, are listed down the left-hand side of the chart.

For each content area, illustrative activities, strategies, or expectancies are detailed under the headings of three developmental levels. Level I is intended to represent the earliest level of exposure to the art, at whatever grade level, consisting largely, though not entirely, of concrete physical information, basic skills, and concepts. Level II reinforces and extends the skills and concepts. Level III is the most advanced, in which synthesis develops on the foundation of the accomplishments of the first two steps, preparing for the students' mature development.

At the same time that concepts are being developed, it is essential, as in *all* teaching, to develop the intrinsic satisfactions inherent in the learning experiences. These are the enduring values that remain when the particulars of specific lessons have been transformed or forgotten. These are the long-term, residual effects, the perceptions, attitudes, enjoyments, understandings, and appreciations that provide the motivation for an individual's extended experiences and continued growth.

Chapter 2

Dance

Dance, the most ancient of arts, has been and still is in some cultures an integral part of religious customs and rituals. It is critical to the socialization process in civilization. Yet, it is only within the twentieth century that dance has had significant growth in higher education and in professional concerts in the United States. Even so, few efforts have been made in educational systems to design a comprehensive developmental sequence of dance education for all students prior to the university or college level.

Dance can make a significant contribution to the curriculum in terms of human development and expression. One rarely stops to think that, before word symbols are learned, infants communicate nonverbally through movement and sound. "Body talk" continues to be a part of human functioning throughout life. Every person has the instrument for dance. Every person acquires an extensive, though nonspecific, movement vocabulary. Motion has purely functional uses and also expressive ones, since every emotional state expresses itself in movement. Anna Halprin, noted dancer and choreographer, says, "In its most basic form, this spontaneous link between movement and feeling consciously ordered is called dance."[1]

In 1976 those attending a nationwide conference on dance in education discussed a rationale for dance in the curriculum and published their conclusions in a book entitled *Dance as Education.*[2] The following ideas are derived from that publication and represent the current philosophy of dance educators in California:

- Dance as a creative experience offers an alternative mode of

---

[1] Anna Halprin, *TAMPLA Institute Training Session, 1980.* Kentfield, Calif.: San Francisco Dancers' Workshop, 1980 (brochure).

[2] Charles B. Fowler, *Dance as Education.* Washington, D.C.: American Alliance for Health, Physical Education, Recreation, & Dance, 1978, pp. 10—14.

expression, with particular emphasis on the felt-component. (*Felt-component* is the basis of intuitive thought; it is the source of movement quality—energy, space, and time.) The experience of improvising and forming movement patterns and compositions leads to the discovery of one's ability to respond with spontaneity and to create aesthetic forms.

- Dance education provides a needed diversity within the school setting by involving the child's physical as well as the mental processes and thereby often reaching children who do not respond easily to verbal approaches alone.
- Dance is one approach to serving the interests of good health. It can add a considerable measure of energetic release and fulfillment to a person's life at the same time as it provides a demanding type of exercise that encourages people to be physically active and fit.
- The dance experience contributes to one's sense of self—personal identification and self-motivation.

- Dance education tends to internalize an understanding of, or an appreciation for, one's own culture and the cultures of other people. It promotes understanding and acceptance of the similarities and differences among races, religions, and cultural traditions.
- Dance can relate to and enhance other academic areas—language arts, mathematics, and the social sciences. The elements of the dance medium—line, pattern, form, space, shape, rhythm, time, and energy—are common to concepts underlying many subjects and, therefore, can contribute to a person's all-around education.

Basic programs in dance should include creative dance for children, modern dance, social dance, and dance of other cultures, especially as related to the local community. Ballet, jazz, and tap dance may be added if they are appropriate to the school setting and available resources.

The student, through participation in a rich and varied dance curriculum throughout the school years, gains in knowledge of the elemental nature, structures, processes, and principles of dance. In addition, experience in both the discipline and creativity of communication through a nonverbal medium leads to a balanced development of the whole person.

The following contents of the framework act as a guide in developing dance curriculum on state, county, and district levels. Each new or redesigned arts/dance program must include multiple dance experiences, along with the other arts, as an integral part of learning. Attention should be given to all sections of the dance framework to build the most comprehensive dance program as is practical and suitable for the individual school, district, or county. The focus is toward growth of the whole person.

Terms in Dance

So that the reader may understand more clearly the terminology used within the chapter, certain terms are defined:

Abstraction—To select the essence of an idea or concept and apply that selection to the art of movement.

Body—Includes body parts and movements. These movements are locomotor (moving from one place to another through space) and axial (contained movement in space around an axis of the body).

Choreography—The art of composing dances.

Creative movement, creative dance—Also referred to sometimes as dance for children, movement education, and movement exploration. Often used interchangeably in the field of dance, but all basically imply the area of dance where movement is primary or nonfunctional, with emphasis on body mastery and discipline for expressive, imaginative, and communicative purposes.

A dance—Rhythmic movement in spatial form; a succession of movement which moves from a beginning to a middle and has an ending. A dance implies the organization of parts in sequential form.

Dance—An all-inclusive term referring to aesthetics of movement; physical movement with expressive intent.

Dance forms—The structure which embodies a choreographed dance.

Dance medium—Body movement. The elements used in movement include space (shape), time (rhythm), and force (energy).

Dance style—A specific manner of performing, showing diversity within a given type or kind of dance characteristic of an individual, a school, a period, a group, or an entire culture.

Dance types or kinds—Categories of dance: ballet, tap, jazz, modern, ethnic, and so forth.

Dance works—Usually referred to as a dance which is choreographed and to be presented in a concert performance.

Dancing—Movement in a "dance-like" way; any coordination and sequencing of movement in a rhythmic ordering.

Exploration—Experiences in sensing, finding, and experimenting with the uses of the elements of movement (space, time, force) in human responses.

Force—Release of potential energy into kinetic energy; an ebb and flow and control of effort. It involves body weight (implied and real), reveals the effects of gravity on the body, is projected into space, and affects motional, emotional, and spatial relationships and intentions.

Improvisation—Movement without previous planning; impromptu movement.

Kinesthetic awareness—Body reaction, muscle memory, and conscious perception of the ability of one's body to "feel" movement.

Modern dance—One of the aesthetic and performance types of creative dance involving specialized movement techniques. With integration of physical and expressive skills, emphasis is on expression and communication. Modern dance has a heritage of various creative approaches.

Movement materials—Movement sequences, motifs, and phrases which can then be developed as the choreographed dance; the inspiration for the creation of movement sequences, motifs, and materials stemming from any source.

Shape—The body always has a shape, but, in the act of designing dance movement, a consciousness is applied to the specific shape/design of the body in motion as well as in moments of stasis.

Space—The immediate space surrounding the body in all directions, as in a sphere; the inner space or space inside the body which can be imaginary as well as that space occupied by the bones, muscles, and so forth; the space in which the body and bodies can move at all levels and distances.

Technique—The physical skills essential to the performer; the integral training of the body for dance.

Time—Movement involving breathing time, emotional time, and metric time (beat, pulse, accent, tempo, duration).

Components, Goals, and Objectives for the Student in Dance Education

The outcomes for student achievement in a dance education program are encompassed in the following components, goals, and objectives.

Component One: Aesthetic Perception—Multisensory Integration

Children have an urge for expressive movement that must be satisfied if their proper development is to be achieved. Dance is an activity in which movement itself is primary, rather than subservient to other goals or purposes. Increasing a student's kinesthetic awareness must be included with the development of the visual, aural, and tactile senses.

Goal I: To develop the student's awareness of the body, a sensing of the communicative potential of body movement, and a capacity for spontaneous movement response

Objective: The student will be able to develop an awareness, identification, and image of the body as an instrument of expression in space and in time.

Goal II: To increase an individual's motor efficiency and kinesthetic sensibility

Objectives: The student will be able to:

1. Respond in movement to sensory stimuli; e.g., sight, sound, and touch.
2. Demonstrate motor efficiency and control and expand movement

vocabulary through dance technique.

3. Verbalize and use movement vocabulary based on the elements of dance fundamentals, integrating the body with space, time, and energy concepts.

Component Two: Creative Expression

Dance, like the other arts, is a medium for personal creativity, including expressing oneself in free and spontaneous movement as well as in guided or structured movement. Through dance an expression of inner feelings, moods, and reactions takes shape as a form. In this process each person's uniqueness and individuality are preserved.

Goal I: To develop the student's ability to express perceptions, feelings, images, and thoughts through dance movement

Objectives: The student will be able to:

1. Communicate personal feelings and ideas through movement with originality, individual style, and clarity.
2. Use improvisation, problem-solving techniques, inventive thinking, and exploration to develop the creative process of dance.
3. Develop an abstract imagery from a variety of sources in composing dances.
4. Select and organize movement into coherent phrases and compositions with organic form and structure.
5. Develop self-evaluation skills related to dance composition and performance.

Goal II: To develop respect for originality in dance

Objectives: The student will be able to:

1. Demonstrate through movement that dance is a form of

communication and that the variety of movement comes from the uniqueness of each individual's expression.
2. Show original movement motifs, phrases, and dance compositions to others in class and in performances.

Component Three: Dance Heritage—Historical and Cultural

Knowledge of dance heritage through the ages is like mapping out the course of civilization. Through the study of dance heritage, knowledge of different styles and forms of dance and the human needs and reasons why people have always danced can be discovered. The social, political, religious, philosophical, and environmental forces that gave birth to the varied dance forms of the world can be relived through the study of dance forms in many cultures.

Goal I: To develop the student's knowledge and appreciation of our multicultural dance heritage

Objectives: The student will be able to:

1. Recognize the dance as a universal language in world cultures—past, present, and future.
2. Articulate the historical roles of dance in relation to social, ritual, and performance contexts.
3. Demonstrate similarities and differences among dance forms from cultural and historical perspectives.

Goal II: To recognize current dance forms and styles and the place of dance in contemporary culture

Objectives: The student will be able to:

1. Articulate the desire to continue active involvement as a spectator or participant in dance at a nonprofessional or professional level.

2. Identify manifestations of dance in contemporary culture within social, ritual, and performance contexts.

Component Four: Aesthetic Valuing

In dance, the development of aesthetic values is inextricably bound up with growth in aesthetic/multisensory perception, creative expression, and understanding of cultural heritage. Although aspects of aesthetic growth may, in many instances, be exhibited through observations and ideas expressed verbally, they are rooted in the movement experiences and creative activities of the dance class. Progress in the development of aesthetic values may be noted in the student's increasing capacity for:

- Enjoyment of movement—concentrated participation in the "doing"
- Observation of movement (one's own and that of others) and remembering of movement performed or observed
- Recognition of form, relationships among movement materials, and interpretation of ideas expressed in movement
- Comment and discussion—making comparisons, recognizing dance styles, evaluating, expressing, and accounting for preferences

Goal I: To develop a sense of involvement, the capacity to enjoy aesthetic expression in dance, and to establish positive attitudes toward self, others, and one's environment

Objectives: The student will be able to:

1. Discover the joy and freedom of creative and uninhibited movement and a wide range of dance experiences.
2. Perceive and value originality in dance compositions, recognizing the uniqueness of oneself and others.

Goal II: To cultivate intellectual bases for making and justifying aesthetic judgments in dance in relation to personal and community values and to the environment

Objectives: The student will be able to:

1. Demonstrate skills of constructive criticism by making judgments about the aesthetic quality of dance works as they relate to communication and to the expression of self, others, and life.
2. Perceive, describe, and compare dance works with respect to their own aesthetic meanings, movement qualities, and the processes used in their creation.
3. Relate the basic elements of dance to the aesthetic qualities of other areas of study.

Developmental Level Charts

The following charts outline program content for development of a curriculum in dance. Rather than being lesson plans, the charts are designed to serve as guidelines in consideration of subject matter content.

Each chart is based on one of the four components of the visual and performing arts curricula. The concepts and content areas in the first column of the chart are interpreted in terms of the possible activities at three progressive levels of experience:

Level I—A beginning stage of learning at any age
Level II—An intermediate stage of learning
Level III—An advanced stage in the dance experience

These suggested content/skill areas and activities are selected samples. They are designed to assist teachers to develop programs that relate both to the content of the discipline and to the interests and abilities of the students. Through the achievement of the objectives mentioned, students may fulfill the goals of the educational program in dance.

Component One: Aesthetic Perception—Multisensory Integration

Goal I: To develop the students' awareness of the body, a sensing of the communicative potential of body movement, and a capacity for spontaneous movement response

Objective: Students will be able to:

• Develop an awareness, identification, and image of the body as an instrument of expression in space and time.

Goal II: To increase an individual's motor efficiency and kinesthetic sensibility

Objectives: The student will be able to:

• Respond in movement to sensory stimuli; e.g., sight, sound, touch.
• Demonstrate motor efficiency and control and expand movement vocabulary through dance technique.
• Verbalize and use movement vocabulary based on the elements of dance fundamentals, integrating the body with space, time, and energy concepts.

Content/Skill	Level I	Level II	Level III
Body awareness	Identify body parts. Explore potential movement in single body parts.	Experience contrast between isolated and whole-body movement.	Experiment with initiating movement in a single body part and allowing it to lead or flow through the whole body.
	Explore movement of body parts in varied combinations.	Observe and follow movement of another person as in follow-the-leader or mirroring activities.	Respond in movement to the movement of another person, as in a movement "conversation."
	Discover different ways in which a natural movement may be executed; describe how the movement feels.	Sense the feeling or tone of movement; respond to the feeling of observed movement.	Find a movement expressive of a mood or feeling; experiment with ways of extending it to make it stronger, clearer, or more emphatic.
	Explore sensory reception in various perceptual modes (sight, sound, tactile, kinesthetic).		
	Respond spontaneously in movement to varied stimuli—a loud sound, a brilliant color, a rough texture, a falling object, and so forth.	Focus attention on kinesthetic sensations with inner "felt" experience of movement.	

Content/Skill	Level I	Level II	Level III
Body awareness (continued)		Experience the perception of the individual related to self, others, and environment.	Demonstrate capacity to experience, express, and communicate feelings through self-created movement and imagery.
Body and self-image	Experience activities to build self-esteem, motivational and positive attitudes.	Experience activities to build self-esteem, imaginative responses,	
		Develop a positive sense of involvement and concentration of attention in movement exploration, expression, and communication.	
Motor efficiency and control	Experience activities that develop gross motor coordination and refined motor control.	Develop awareness of body alignment and balance while increasing other physical aspects of strength, flexibility, agility, and endurance.	Perform movements more demanding of technical skill.
	Experience developmental stages of locomotor and axial movement and natural body coordinations (opposition, peripheral, central).	Increase awareness and identification of body movement potential, care, and injury prevention.	Demonstrate knowledge of physiological and kinesiological principles and body integration techniques.
Space	Explore through body movements: personal space, contained space, space of others.	Demonstrate a sense of relationship to surrounding space combining spatial concepts with time and energy concepts.	Utilize personal space, "stage" space, relationship with others, directions, levels, range, and pathways in movement expression.
	Kinesthetically explore spatial concepts: levels, directions, dimensions, and paths.		

Content/Skill	Level I	Level II	Level III
Space (continued)	Explore making body shapes, lines, angles, and curves.	Demonstrate ability to relate body with spatial designs; make body shapes, lines, angles, curves, and designs.	Experiment with individual and group shapes and spatial designs.
Time	Identify time concepts through movement experience: fast/slow, long/short, sudden/sustained.	Demonstrate ability to perceive and perform movement based on duple and triple meters and tempi varied in relation to a basic pulse.	Perform movement phrases with more complex rhythmic and metrical structures.
	Explore internal rhythms of the body through movement: pulse, breath, gait.		
Force	Explore amount of force in movement by flow and control of energy and weight.	Demonstrate awareness of internal force (tensions within physical structure of body).	
	Explore range of tension and release on body.	Demonstrate awareness of external force (tensions created by gravitational pull on body).	
	Develop ability to differentiate various amounts of weight and force in movements against gravity or other outside forces.	Demonstrate sensitivity to range of movement qualities (sustained, percussive, vibratory, swing).	
	Explore range of energy flow in personal movement style.		
	Explore qualities of movement plus rhythm.		Demonstrate a sense of dynamic flow and organization of kinesthetic tensions through uses of force in phrasing of movement expression.

Component Two: Creative Expression

Goal I: To develop the student's ability to express perceptions, feelings, images, and thoughts through dance movement

Objectives: The student will be able to:

- Communicate personal feelings and ideas through movement with originality, individual style, and clarity.
- Use improvisation, problem-solving techniques, inventive thinking, and exploration to develop the creative process of dance.
- Transform an abstract imagery from a variety of sources in composing dances.
- Select and organize movement into coherent phrases and compositions with organic form and structure.
- Develop self-evaluation skills related to dance composition and performance.

Goal II: To develop respect for orginality in dance

Objectives: The student will be able to:

- Demonstrate through movement that dance is a form of communication and that the variety of movement comes from the uniqueness of each individual's expression.
- Show original movement motifs, phrases, and dance compositions to others in class and in performances.

Content/Skill	Level I	Level II	Level III
Improvisation	Discover motivations for movement improvisation from auditory, tactile, visual, and motor stimuli, emotional states, textures, shapes, concepts, and ideas.		Incorporate many stimuli within the structure of an improvisation, and move with spontaneity and clarity of expression.
	Move in quick, spontaneous, individual responses relating to changing stimuli.	Improvise with a clear focus within a simple structure, individually or in groups.	
Abstraction	Use sources and imagery for abstraction from gestures, emotions, characters, nature, animals, universal themes, words, literature, poetry, dramatic themes, and other dance forms.		Create a dance about an experience or feeling that projects the abstracted image into a clearly articulated form.
	Improvise movement based on a feeling or in response to an imagined situation.	Transform movement from pantomimic representation to abstracted illusion and imagery.	

Content/Skill	Level I	Level II	Level III
Craft of choreography	Create a simple dance with a beginning, a middle section, and an ending. Design movement in space. Originate a simple rhythm pattern in sound and movement. Create a repeatable movement sequence.	Organize and develop movement through space designs, time patterns, and dynamic flow into structured sequences, phrases, and sections. Create short dance studies based on problems posed in the learning of various aspects of the craft of choreography.	Develop an original dance with conscious use of all aspects of craft within the motivation and intent of the choreography.
Elements of form	Use elements of variety, contrast, and repetition in movement explorations. Create short dance studies based on simple musical forms: two-part, ABA, round.	Add elements of balance, sequence, harmony, transition, climax, and unity to dance composition. Evaluate own and others' dances according to criteria based on assigned problem and the elements of form. Create dance forms using rondo, theme and variations, sonata, fugue, canon, and free forms.	
Self-evaluation	Observe own success in the suggested creative exploration.	Observe and discuss own success in handling assigned movement sequences.	Use self-evaluation to rework dances.
Performance	Show dance movement in classroom and other appropriate environments.	Perform informally at assemblies and other school or community functions. Add costumes, sets, props, film, or video to choreography as may be applicable.	Participate in concert performances and productions.

Component Three: Dance Heritage—Historical and Cultural

Goal I: To develop the student's knowledge and appreciation of our multicultural dance heritage

Objectives: The student will be able to:

- Recognize dance as a universal language in world cultures—past, present, and future.
- Articulate the historical roles of dance in relation to social, ritual, and performance contexts.
- Demonstrate similarities and differences of dance forms from cultural and historical perspectives.

Goal II: To recognize current dance forms and styles and the place of dance in contemporary culture

Objectives: The student will be able to:

- Articulate the desire to continue active involvement as a spectator or participant in dance at a nonprofessional or professional level.
- Identify manifestations of dance in contemporary culture within social, ritual, and performance contexts.

Content/Skill	Level I	Level II	Level III
Historical and cultural context of dance	Recognize that dance has a past, present, and future.	Identify the place of dance as a means of communication throughout human history.	Investigate why humans dance.
	Identify dance styles from a variety of cultures.	Identify and compare dance styles from historical and cultural perspectives.	
	Identify universal themes and values represented in dance in various cultures.		
	Develop reading and observation of historical or cultural dance.		
		Compare dance as theatre performance and as cultural expression.	
	Study dances from various periods in history.	Relate and compare dance and other arts in various periods of history.	
		Identify major dance innovators and their contributions throughout history.	

Content/Skill	Level I	Level II	Level III
Historical and cultural context of dance (continued)	Explore heritage and cross-cultural influences on the development of dance forms.		Articulate the place of dance and movement in social contexts in selected cultures. Study western culture dance which evolved into ballet, jazz, tap, and social forms.
Dance in contemporary culture as recreation or vocation	Realize that dance is a part of everyday life. Participate as a spectator of dance.		Realize that dance activity can be continued throughout life. Recognize the place of dance in current social contexts. Differentiate between dance as a profession and dance as an avocation or a recreation. Identify dance in contemporary culture and its roles in leisure-time activities, health, and social activities. Know the diverse career directions available in dance. Know the private and public institutions for continuing study of dance.

Component Four: Aesthetic Valuing—Enjoyment, Observation, Recognition, Comment

Goal I: To develop a sense of involvement, the capacity to enjoy aesthetic expression in dance, and to establish positive attitudes toward self, others, and one's environment

Objectives: The student will be able to:

- Discover the joy and freedom of creative and uninhibited movement and a wide range of dance experiences.
- Perceive and value originality in dance compositions, recognizing the uniqueness of oneself and others.

Goal II: To cultivate intellectual bases for making and justifying aesthetic judgments in dance in relation to personal and community values and to the environment

Objectives: The student will be able to:

- Demonstrate skills of constructive criticism and make judgments about the aesthetic quality of dance works as they relate to communication and to expression of self, others, and life.
- Perceive, describe, and compare dance works with respect to their own aesthetic meanings, movement qualities, and the processes used in their creation.
- Relate the basic elements of dance to the aesthetic qualities of other areas of study.

In the following tables, components one, two, and three are identified as the content of the aesthetic valuing component. Expectancies for each of these content categories have been drawn from the table specific to each of the first three components. The aesthetic values provided by the expectancies at the three developmental levels are designated in the four following catetories:

- Enjoyment of movement
- Observation of movement
- Recognition of form
- Comment and discussion

Content/Skill	Level I	Level II	Level III
Aesthetic perception	Develop body awareness, motor efficiency, kinesthetic sensitivity through movement, exploration, growth in skills, and sensory experiences in all perceptual modes.		
	Enjoyment of engaging in rhythmic movement of the whole body	Enjoyment of doing a wide range of movements of varying qualities	Enjoyment of doing both simple and more difficult movement, and longer, more complex phrases
	Observation of others' movement, verbalizing of observations	Observation of own and others' movement, remembering movement	Observation and remembering of movement motifs and phrases

Content/Skill	Level I	Level II	Level III
Aesthetic perception (continued)		Recognition, through kinesthetic response, of expressive values in varied movement materials	Recognition of expression through movement as related to various sensory experiences or suggested imagery
		Comment upon observations and reactions	Comment upon observations, comparing movement materials, noting individual ways of moving
Creative expression	Experience the creative process of dance through the discovery of original movement and the organization of movement into forms capable of communicating individual feelings or ideas.		
	Enjoyment of spontaneous motor response to varied stimuli	Enjoyment of improvising singly, with partners, or in groups; of performing set phrases with accuracy and clarity	Enjoyment of wide variety of improvisations, of composing and performing phrases and whole dances with clarity and projection
	Observation of improvisations of others	Observation of others' improvisations and dances, remembering one's own dances	Remembering one's own dances and one's perceptions of dances observed
	Interpretation of meaning in movement	Recognition of formal structure of composed or observed dances; interpretation of meaning in movement	Recognition and analysis of dance form, noting relationship and manipulation of movement materials
			Interpretation of dance meaning
	Verbalization of reactions	Comment on observed dances in terms of choice of movement, form, and communication	Discussion of unique points of observed dance, success of communication, styles of movement
		Comparisons among dances	Substantiation of evaluations and preferences

Content/Skill	Level I	Level II	Level III
Dance heritage	Build up knowledge and understanding of dance—its history, its roles in society, its variety as related to cultural context, and its numerous contemporary styles and forms—through learning steps, patterns, and dances of different historical or cultural situations; viewing dances (film and live performance); reading; discussing; and composing dances related to historical or cultural material.		
	Enjoyment of doing steps and simple patterns of dances of various forms and styles	Enjoyment of doing dances of different periods and cultures	Enjoyment of performing historical or ethnic dances, or dances based on authentic sources
	Observation of a variety of historical and ethnic dances	Observation of dances in performance	Observation of a wide variety of traditional dances
		Recall of dances observed	Recall of dances learned and observed
		Recognition of form of historical or diverse cultural dances	Recognition of form of authentic dances or those based on authentic sources, relating movement to historical or cultural origins basic to understanding or interpretation of the dances
		Interpretation of dances in relation to historical or cultural contexts	
		Comment: comparing dances, identifying styles, stating and accounting for preferences	Comment: comparing dances as to movement, form, and meaning; noting styles; stating and accounting for preferences

Program Development

Those developing a dance education program need to consider the following essential aspects of such a program: curriculum planning, student performances, teacher preparation, in-service training, and community resources.

Curriculum Planning

The educational values and personal benefits to students who have participated in dance programs have become increasingly apparent in the past decade. The National Endowment for the Arts developed model residency programs nationwide during that period.

The first step in curriculum planning is for each school within each district to develop and maintain its own dance education program, preschool through high school.

Such comprehensive curriculum planning should be based on primary guidelines for developing a dance education program:

- Extend the programs from the preschool through the high school levels.
- Exhibit a balance between creative activity and dance skills development.
- Devise a sequential programming of courses and experiences.
- Make the program accessible to all students at every grade level.
- Ensure the availability of space, time, and facilities to serve program needs.
- Include consistent and adequate time blocks weekly for dance classes.
- Relate to an overall philosophical framework and well-defined goals in dance.
- Provide opportunities for active learning through dance experience.
- Provide a plan for systematic evaluation of program effectiveness.

The *Visual and Performing Arts Framework* should be used for more detailed content development of the dance program. The skills and energies of teachers, principals, parents, community members, and dance professionals should be available to make contributions to the dance education program as related to the framework.

Student Performances

To know dance as a performing art, students must both participate in and observe performances. Student performance in dance is not the dominant goal of the total dance curriculum, but it is part of the learning process of and about dance and, as such, is a significant culmination which encompasses creating, practicing, and working with others. It is an experience of educational value and aesthetic pleasure for both the performer and audience and is a means of conveying the art of dance as a nonverbal experience and discipline.

Inventive and careful planning should allow beginning performing experiences to be shared experiences rather than "show" activities, thus

avoiding exploitation of the students and distortion of the educational dance program. These performances should be an outgrowth of the students' capacity to move expressively at a level of excellence compatible with their age and potential and thus should avoid the tendency to produce high-powered performances with a selected few students. Dance material should be appropriate for the level, skill, particular learning situation, knowledge, and understanding of both the participants and the audience.

At first, performances should provide for informal presentations in the classroom or studio. This approach can offer the student performers an opportunity to share a newly acquired skill; demonstrate their solution to a problem; or evaluate a particular experience in dance with their class, other classes, or an invited audience, such as parents.

The next step should provide for more formal dance presentations as students become more skilled and audiences more attuned. In the process, performances should allow for interrelation with, and take advantage of, the expertise of the other arts.

Teacher Preparation

To carry out the goals, objectives, content, and expectancies in this visual and performing arts framework, the state should require additional courses in dance in the preparation of teachers for elementary and secondary levels. As an arts discipline and a subject area basic to the classroom teaching and learning process, K—12, dance should be included in the core of courses required of the single- and multiple-subjects credential program in colleges and universities. Provisions must be made to develop teacher competency in all the arts in education. Since dance is the most recent of arts disciplines to be incorporated in a state curriculum framework, action should be taken to ensure adequate teacher education through course work in the basic body of knowledge and teaching methods in dance.

Examples of course work in teacher preparation curriculum for credentials in preschool, early childhood education, special education, general elementary, and multiple subjects are:

- Content and methods of creative dance/movement exploration for children
- Modern dance technique and composition
- Human development and experiential learning, movement concepts, and approaches to teaching young children
- Classroom subject areas taught through dance

At the secondary level, teacher preparation should include course work leading to a single-subject dance credential, such as the dance major or minor, as established by *Standards for Dance Major Programs*.[3] For dance specialists, teacher preparation curriculum should include courses outlined above for both elementary and secondary levels. Even with these educational goals in mind, a successful teacher in dance must have the willingness and openness to provide, with spirit and commitment, opportunities for students to explore dance and expression. The teacher needs to be in a continual process of learning and acquiring tools and understanding for greater effectiveness within the discipline.

The dance teacher in kindergarten through grade six should achieve basic competencies in:

- Leading children in expressing and experiencing dance through structured improvisation and creative problem-solving
- Knowing and teaching the basic elements of the dance and movement medium, including social and cultural dance forms

---

[3]*Standards for Dance Major Programs*. Edited by Alma Hawkins. Los Angeles: Council of Dance Administrators, 1979.

- Perceiving and reinforcing children's involvement and responsiveness in their dance experience
- Teaching classroom subject areas through dance and integrating all arts concepts
- Providing vivid learning opportunities in dance through tapping school and community dance resources

The dance teacher at the secondary level should achieve basic competencies in:

- Providing a stimulating learning environment, whether it be in the fine arts or in a physical education setting, or both
- Structuring and teaching dance technique classes appropriate to the students' skill levels, needs, and interests
- Guiding group dance improvisation and composition
- Evaluating student competency and heightening student perception of aesthetic values in performance viewed in class and in professional concerts
- Initiating interrelationships among arts classes in the school
- Recognizing and challenging talented and gifted dance students by referral to other special learning environments and opportunities

In-service Training

So that students may take advantage of the value and benefits of dance in education, school systems must provide in-service teacher training. Many teachers need to be more adequately trained in the dance discipline. A dance teacher at any level should be able to implement the curriculum outlined in this framework.

Students who are training to become elementary-level school teachers are not required to take college and university dance education classes as part of the current multiple-subjects credential. Therefore, most elementary school teachers must

depend on in-service staff development workshops, survey classes, and/or the sharing of methods with other teachers.

Until training in dance becomes mandatory for all who seek the multiple-subjects credential, school administrators should make every effort to employ a dance specialist or coordinator who can oversee and direct planning and instruction to implement the dance curriculum. This person would be responsible for conducting in-service training for staff development as well as for coordinating resource consultants from within the community.

If school districts, because of budgeting and financial improbabilities, cannot hire a dance specialist or coordinator, the administration has the responsibility to provide for the teachers' continual professional growth in dance. Teachers should be encouraged to enroll in dance courses in local colleges and universities, and they should be provided with opportunities to participate in special workshops offered for their professional development in dance.

Because dance is both a physical discipline and a performing art, it should be offered at the secondary level in the fine arts curriculum or in both fine arts and physical education. Ideally, each school should employ at least one dance teacher who is capable of teaching the skills and the art of dance.

Community Resources

For dance to be accessible to all students as an on-going part of their educational experience, community members need to see that the schools include dance in their curricula. Within the community are numerous opportunities for extension of dance knowledge and experience and a sense of dance as a vital part of community life.

The following outline indicates a diversity of community resources for dance in relation to persons and organizations, places, and funding resources for dance.

Certain individuals and organizations may be able to provide expertise in a specific area of dance. One of the most valuable resources for dance instruction is person-to-person communication through:

- Local artists or specialists
- Community services, such as the local university, college, junior college, or recreation department
- National Endowment for the Arts, Washington, D.C. (The dance component functions as a part of the Artists-in-the-Schools program under the NEA. A school district may request this program from the NEA.)
- Dance Organizations:
  1. California Dance Educators Association (CDEA)
  2. California Association of Health, Physical Education, Recreation, and Dance (CAHPERD)
  3. Los Angeles Area for Dance Alliance (LAADA)
  4. Bay Area Dance Coalition, San Francisco
  5. American Alliance of Health, Physical Education, Recreation, and Dance (AAHPERD)
  6. National Dance Association (NDA) (under AAHPERD)
  7. Congress on Research in Dance (CORD)
  8. American Dance Guild (ADG)

The following are places within a community for dance education to occur:

- City and county educational resource centers
- Parks and recreation centers
- Performing arts centers
- Museums and galleries
  1. Space for classes, performances, lectures, or films
  2. Interrelated activities

- Malls, churches, libraries
  1. Space for classes, performances, lectures, or films
  2. Interrelated activities
- Field trips
  1. Concerts
  2. Master classes
  3. Lectures or demonstrations
  4. Library or museum displays

Funding resources may be available from the following:

- Business corporations in the community
- Grants from:
  1. California Arts Council (CAC)
  2. National Endowment for the Arts (NEA)
  3. National Endowment for the Humanities (NEH)
- Museums or galleries

Students with Special Needs

Dance education can benefit special students by offering them substantial assistance in reaching their full potential.

The particular ways that dance can help the special student are as follows:

- Increase the self-esteem of an individual from success at doing and/or creating movement by oneself and performing it for others.
- Release psychophysical tension or academic stress with movement catharsis.
- Appreciate and accept the uniqueness of individuals through the sharing of the dance experience.
- Perceive and/or create dances leading to intrinsic aesthetic enjoyment.
- Develop and enhance body image and spatial concepts which support learning in other curriculum areas.
- Provide experiential learning for students whose learning styles are nonanalytical and nonverbal, as essential to cognitive achievement.

- Provide for an individualized approach within a group setting.

For gifted and talented students, expression and communication through dance are not so much particular learnings of skills but are essentially ways for exploring self—feelings, body, and environment.

A student talented in dance may demonstrate a variety of characteristics and possess some, not necessarily all, of the capacities listed as follows:

- Flexibility and control of body as an instrument for expression
- Use of the body, with confidence, as an instrument of expression, self-identification, and pleasure
- Manipulation of movement, energy flows, rhythm, and spatial and body design to express feeling and meaning through the dance image
- Development of sensitivity to a range of energies which can produce a full scope of expressive forces in movement imagery production

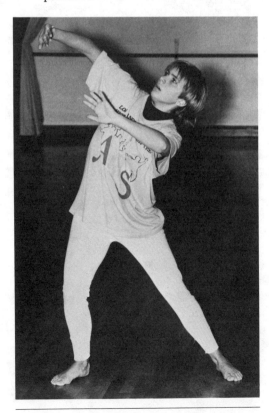

- Movement timing, which creates rhythmic structure and dynamic forces in the dance image
- Space ordering to enhance meaningful expression of ideas or feelings in the creation of spatial design and illusion as forces in the dynamic dance image
- Expression of feeling and meaning with originality and aesthetic sensibility

Some students will excel in the development of the body as an instrument for dance, and others will

develop highly creative competency in conceptual-choreographic ability. These are the paths of the performer and the choreographer. Students usually show a tendency for excellence in one of these directions. In the initial course of their development, the intellectually gifted students, though not necessarily talented in dance, can gain immeasurably in the balancing of their capacities for physical, emotional, and intellectual growth through dance experience.

In providing dance experience for students gifted and talented in dance, teachers should:

- Expand the student's frame of reference through contact with new ideas, experiences, and materials.
- Enrich the environment for learning with materials related to dance—books, video, film, concerts, and contact with artists and resource people.
- Encourage risk-taking and experimentation in new areas of dance experience.
- Encourage fulfillment of creative projects and developing interests.
- Show responsiveness and appreciation for dance studies.
- Recognize and reinforce intuitive awareness of students, and share relevant insights and concepts.

Multicultural Education

The dance experience is an ideal instrument for developing and enriching bilingual and multicultural programs because dance is a nonverbal medium. Participation in dances of other cultures enables the student to experience feelings, sensations, and ideas associated with those cultures—in a way "to see through the eyes of another." Such techniques constitute a valuable means for helping young people learn how to live in peace, harmony, and mutual respect in a complex, pluralistic society.

Each age is mirrored in its art. Dance students can sense the rich contributions of the multiethnic and multicultural groups, past and present, which make up the American heritage. They will realize how the common past, as well as personal experience, has been captured and preserved and recreated for new audiences in terms of recreational, social, aesthetic, and theatrical dance. In fact, students, through their own dance work, can make creative contributions to their changing culture.

From basic awarenesses explored through dance education, the culturally mixed student body of our

American public schools can achieve recognition of differences in cultural interpretations. Each student then will experience, through dance, how each culture created its own dance forms, influenced by religion, philosophy, politics, medicine, health, environment, and attitudes of an individual as a social being. In the learning of dances of each culture represented by the students in the class, ceremonial, recreational, theatrical, and social dances can be explored and explained. The teacher, in the role of a facilitator, is able to illustrate how basic American dance education relates to all cultural forms of dance.

Careers in Dance

In addition to experiencing dance in the educational setting, a student should learn the carry-over value for future use in dance as a profession. A wide range of careers exists in the field. Throughout the grade levels, a curriculum in dance would sustain the student's ability to dance through student involvement, progress, and growth. This curriculum also should motivate those with talent and interest toward career directions in dance and related areas. The chief opportunities for such careers are through five avenues:

1. Professional performance (modern dance, ethnic dance, ballet, jazz, theatrical dance)
   Performer
   Choreographer

2. Technical and administrative support
   Designer (lighting, costumes, props, sets)
   Stage manager
   Composer/musician
   Business manager and public relations representative
   Notation specialist
   Photographer
   Film/video specialist

3. Education
   Dance educator (K—12 and higher education)
   Educator or educational consultant (dance programs in public and private schools; dance movement for athletes, gymnasts, skaters, actors, and participants in other art and physical education areas; children's programs outside the schools; and theatrical dance training; health programs and special education)
   Operator of private dance studio (owner and/or teacher)
   Dance therapy (public and private institutions, private practice)

4. Recreation
   Parks and recreation programs, such as classes in folk and ethnic dance, jazz, tap, ballet, and geriatrics classes (YMCA, YWCA, health clubs)
   Recreational instructor of fitness

5. Criticism and Research
   Writer/critic
   Historian/researcher
   Ethnologist

Assessment of Progress

Student development in dance occurs along a continuum which is traversed at varying rates. By observing a student's work over a period of time (a term or a year), a teacher can discern both subjective and objective aspects of the progress made. Evaluation should be based on the individual's growth and development in dance in relation to skill levels, conceptual understanding, and ability to formalize dance expression. Progress can be more easily identified in the context of the processes which comprise the student's dance experience. These two processes are:

- Originating movement themes, phrases, or dances and performing them for the expression of individual feelings, ideas, and moods
- Responding to the movement expression of others

Originating and expressing can be observed in the student's ability to:

- Select appropriate movement, which has personal qualities or significance.
- Vary, develop, and relate movements in a logical manner.
- Construct coherent movement phrases.
- Relate personal experiential sources to outward expressive forms through unique and original movement.

- Demonstrate technical skill in the execution of movement.
- Dance with concentration, purpose, and care.

Aspects of responding that can provide indications of progress are the student's ability to:

- Observe movement carefully, remember that movement, and describe it verbally or recreate it in movement.
- Note similarities and differences among movements, phrases, or dances, and discuss these comparisons in terms of both movement itself and its meaning or subject matter.
- Discern structuring of movement into phrases, sections, and whole dances and sequencing into beginning, middle, and end.
- Recognize various styles of dance and their personal or cultural characteristics.
- Respond to dance performance in terms of describing reactions, stating preferences, and accounting for opinions or judgments.

For assessment of progress in dance, various methods or tools may be utilized by the teacher and also for self-evaluation by the student. Examples are:

- Observations (by self, other students, teacher)
- Discussions
- Demonstrations of successful solution of problems in movement

discovery or the creating of dance phrases and/or complete dance compositions

- Tests, quizzes, reports on dance and related subjects
- Performances—informally in the classroom or formally on stage or other performance spaces
- Use of audiovisual equipment (videotaping) to preserve the "moment" of the "dance image" and its movement content for viewing, responding, and evaluating at a later time

Environment, Materials, and Equipment

To have a quality program in dance education, program planners must give their attention to the location, materials, and equipment. Dance is unique in that adequate open, cleared floor space must be provided. However, each dance situation is special. Creative planning, adjustment, and selection are required to provide the optimum environment and materials, as specified in the following sections.

Selection Guidelines

School districts should plan to make sufficient and appropriate materials and supplies available to teachers and students. Since this document does not provide criteria for selection of instructional materials and supplies in dance, school districts can establish guidelines and principles to

aid in their selection of supplies and materials.

A committee should be established to search out, evaluate, and select materials for the basic needs of dance. At the present time supplemental supplies in most schools are inadequate. If care in selection and patience in seeking resources are used, excellent films, books, and other materials can be found. The hope is that, with the adoption of this framework, more books, textbooks, films, videotapes, slides, instruments for accompaniment, records, and music for dance will be forthcoming.

A committee for setting criteria and making the actual selection of materials will give attention to the following procedures:

- Seek out district philosophy and goals for dance education; or, if none exist, strongly recommend and promote formulation of philosophy, goals, and objectives for dance education.
- Conduct a needs survey for dance education programs in the schools within a district.
- Establish criteria for selection of supplies and materials for dance education.

Environment

The environment most favorable to learning in dance consists of three interdependent elements:

- Institutional attitudes. These involve a district and school in

which dance is regarded as a vital part of education and which, through curricular structures and scheduling arrangements, makes dance activities available to every student at every grade level.

- Classroom atmosphere. Teachers should use materials and procedures that will achieve the goals and objectives described in this framework.
- Physical facilities. Dance can take place in a classroom lacking appropriate physical facilities; but to be successful, a program needs a "dancing place" which provides real space of an appropriate size, design, and construction for vigorous dance activities. Those responsible should ensure that dance takes place on resilient wood surfaces. Safety factors must be considered, as well as the adaptability of the space to varying aspects of dance education. Storage space for materials and equipment is needed, and, at the secondary level, dressing space.

For maximum learning in dance, all three of these environmental elements must be favorable. An absence or serious deficiency in any one of them could so limit or weaken the dance program as to make its educational goals not attainable.

Materials and Equipment

The following is a list of materials and equipment which will assist the teacher in presenting dance experiences:

1. Musical instruments:
   - Percussion instruments (drums, gongs, rattles, wood blocks, bells, xylophones, rhythm sticks, tambourines, and so forth) are essential. Since almost everyone is able to use percussion instruments, they are very useful in rhythmic training, with locomotor activities, and in connection with student dance

compositions. They can be very expensive, but a small supply of "real instruments" can be supplemented with usable sound-making objects found around the home or classroom or with instruments made by the students themselves. Having enough instruments of one sort or another is advisable so that each student will have something to play during percussion activities.
   - Recorders or other small wind instruments are helpful.
   - A piano is standard equipment and a necessity in most dance studios. Even a teacher without a regular accompanist can use the piano when students are working on movement qualities, rythmic materials, phrasing, and so forth.

2. Instructional media that are useful include record player, tape recorder, motion picture projector, slide projector, and videotape equipment. Although it is often difficult to coordinate recorded music with dance activities where movement changes frequently, where phrases are short and irregular, or where meters vary, the record player can be very useful in teaching dances with set patterns, such as folk dances or tap dances. Recorded music can provide a basis for movement improvisation, an avenue for experiencing meters, accents, dynamics, phrasing, and other qualities. It can also be a means for students to grasp dance-music relationships. Through motion pictures and slides, students can increase their knowledge of dance of other periods and places, as well as have contact with dance works of our own time. The videotape enables students to see themselves in action. This is particularly relevant to older students who are eager to improve their technical skills or who are preparing dances for presentation.

3. Books and prints available should include books on dance history and dance in other cultures, biographies of dancers, costume books, myths and stories, and art books. Pictures of dancers and dances, costumes, action (sports, work, animals, machines), historical scenes, and designs are important as source materials. A collection of musical scores and songs is needed to provide a basis for even very elementary improvisation or choreography.

4. Miscellaneous equipment important for the dance place should include mirrors and barres, boxes and levels. A metronome is helpful.

5. Materials of various sorts useful for improvisation and composition work are essential: scarves, streamers, balls, balloons, paper bags, newspapers, ropes, elastics, costume items (e.g., hats, capes, skirts, jackets), crayons, paper, pieces of fabric, and masks.

Any of these many and infinitely varied teaching aids is just that—an *aid*—not a substitute for excellence in dance instruction. When a fine teaching and learning situation exists, teaching aids can increase the teacher's resources to extend and enrich each student's dance experience.

Conclusion to Chapter 2

Inherent to the individual's learning in dance is a belief that the body is a matrix of experience—a center for immediate and direct exploration of medium and materials. The body allows a feeling-thinking integration in human experience and becomes a nonverbal, experiential channel to feed academic achievement.

Students, through participation in a rich and varied dance curriculum throughout their school years, gain in knowledge of the elemental nature, structures, processes, and principles of dance. In addition, experience in both the discipline and creativity of communication through a nonverbal medium leads to a balanced development of the whole person. Dance is more than physical movement. It is aesthetic. It is knowing, feeling, and expressing the revelation of self and of life.

Chapter 3

Drama/Theatre

Drama and theatre are subject disciplines which emphasize the use of the intellect as well as the development of a person's sensitivity, creativity, and the capacity to make reasoned, aesthetic decisions while extending the range of human experience. Because drama is concerned with the uniqueness of the individual, students who are guided in drama and theatre activities acquire knowledge of and regard for themselves and others as individuals. These disciplines develop within the student a positive self-concept, creative thinking, and an ability to perceive and interact successfully with others.

Since drama has language as its primary component, students involved in drama/theatre programs develop poise, confidence, ease, and versatility in verbal presentation. Drama/theatre, when taught as a subject discipline, develops the creative, critical, and communicative potential of all students. Drama/theatre education needs to be a regular offering at all grade levels. Students are interested in drama, and, when given the opportunity to participate in theatrical activity, respond with vigor and dedication. It is a powerful subject for enriching the entire curriculum.

This chapter provides information on the scope and the role that drama/theatre can play in the elementary and secondary schools. It is meant to assist administrators, curriculum and drama/theatre specialists, and teachers in their development and supervision of a quality drama/theatre program. This material will prove useful in creating new programs, evaluating existing programs, or expanding and improving current drama/theatre programs.

Terms in Drama/Theatre

So that coherence and cohesiveness will be maintained throughout this chapter on drama, certain terms, as

they are used here, are defined for the reader:

Acting—A cumulative and culminating experience, acting involves sensory awareness, rhythm and movement, pantomime, oral communication, improvisation, and playmaking. It requires careful preparation and rehearsal of scripted theatre literature which leads to a performance before an audience. (Acting is not suggested for any but secure students under the guidance of a specifically trained teacher-director.)

Drama—Used broadly, the term *drama* involves the reenactment of life situations for entertainment or for the purpose of understanding oneself and others. Drama is a process geared to the participant and does not require a formal audience.

Improvisation—Based on individualized response, improvisation involves creative, cooperative, spontaneous, and flexible response to rapidly changing and unanticipated dramatic stimuli. It involves problem solving with no preconception of how to perform, permitting everything in the environment (animate or inanimate) to serve the experience.

Playmaking—A consciously planned and structured activity, playmaking is original story improvisation that is carefully structured and planned, played, evaluated, and replayed with no formal audience.

Theatre—Geared to the audience, theatre includes drama and activities which may lead to the formal presentation of a scripted play involving acting, directing, designing, managing, and other technical aspects.

Processes of Drama/Theatre

The primary educational goal of drama/theatre is the development of each student's imagination and problem-solving and communicative potential. Through an increasing engagement in dramatic processes, students experience theatre; and through their increasing grasp of dramatic concepts, they understand theatre.

The processes of drama/theatre are the avenues by which the student experiences and thus develops concepts about the art. Engagement in the processes of originating, performing and producing, and responding develops an individual's capacities which underlie all creative dramatic activity—concentrating, listening, observing, replacing, remembering, imagining, feeling, recognizing, differentiating, experimenting, and evaluating.

Originating and Performing

The teacher provides stimuli to arouse the imagination, sharpen sensory perception, and generate engagement in expressive activity. Goals are set to focus and give coherence, purpose, and meaning to the creative act. Areas included are sensory and emotional awareness, rhythm and movement, pantomime, oral communication, improvisation, playmaking/playwriting, formal acting, and designing.

Producing

Producing should not be understood in the limited context of formal presentation to an audience. Rather, it includes any interpretative experience in drama/theatre, formal or informal, such as directing, managing, and executing technical elements.

Responding

No drama/theatre experience is complete until it has been subject to the process of reflection. Assessment of the experience in terms of agreed upon criteria is important to the development of concepts about the art and the refinement of critical skills. Traditional criteria for evaluation include:

Intent—The objective, purpose, theme, message, basic idea, or "spine" of a drama/theatre work.

Structure—The interaction between all the components of a work. It includes the elements of design, unity, coherence, emphasis, rhythm, harmony, climax, conflict, transition, contrast, stress, balance, and sequence.

Effectiveness—The means whereby a drama/theatre work entertains, interests, informs, illuminates, inspires, persuades, elates, surprises, stimulates, excites, moves, engages, amuses, delights, shocks, or awes an audience.

Worth—The profundity, validity, or amount of knowledge, intelligence, wisdom, insight, or feeling present or evident in a work.

Regardless of whether students maintain any other artistic skills acquired during their education, the art of responding should enrich an entire lifetime.

Components, Goals, and Objectives for the Student in Drama/Theatre Education

The outcomes for student achievement in a drama/theatre education program are encompassed in the following components, goals, and objectives.

Component One: Aesthetic Perception—Multisensory Integration

Goal I: To experience dramatic elements, actions, and characterizations

Objectives: The student will be able to:

1. Become perceptive and selective in observing and responding to the environment.
2. Use movement as the external expression of an internal idea, intention, or feeling.
3. Use the voice as an instrument for the expression of meaning and feeling, whether in speech or nonverbal sound.

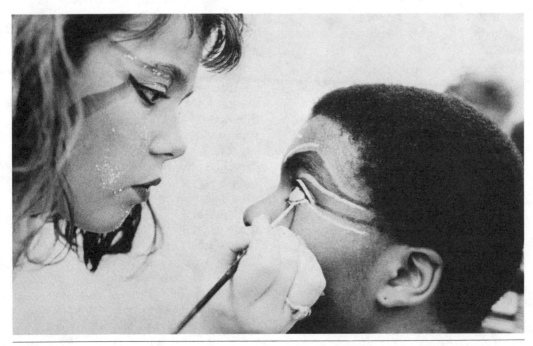

4. Respond spontaneously and collaboratively to rapidly changing, unanticipated stimuli.

Component Two: Creative Expression

Goal I: To develop skills in storytelling, playmaking, and playwriting

Objectives: The student will be able to:

1. Retell and perform a story.
2. Perform an improvisation which is structured, played, evaluated, and replayed.
3. Write original scenes or plays from improvisations.
4. Create appropriate design and technical elements for such scenes or plays.

Goal II: To develop an awareness of the collaborative nature of playmaking

Objectives: The student will be able to:

1. Participate actively in the planning of a dramatization.
2. Perform group dramatizations.
3. Evaluate group effort in exploring and expressing ideas.

Goal III: To develop acting skills for theatrical performance

Objectives: The student will be able to:

1. Become proficient in basic acting skills.
2. Use basic elements of formal acting: characterization, conflict, motivation, and setting.
3. Acquire basic vocabulary related to formal acting.

Goal IV: To develop an awareness of the collaborative nature of theatre and the many skills needed to prepare a finished production

Objectives: The student will be able to:

1. Learn directing.
2. Learn stage managing.
3. Learn business managing; e.g., publicity, box office.

4. Learn design and technical elements of sets, lights, costumes, props, sound, and special effects.
5. Understand how other art forms, such as music, dance, visual arts, and literature, are used in drama/theatre.

Component Three: Drama/Theatre Heritage — Historical and Cultural

Goal I: To develop a knowledge of and appreciation for drama/theatre heritage

Objectives: The student will be able to:

1. Recognize major themes, historical periods, and cultural backgrounds.
2. Recognize the importance of today's theatre as a means of understanding and appreciating cultural differences.

Component Four: Aesthetic Valuing

Goal I: To develop a system of aesthetic valuing of drama/theatre

Objectives: The student will be able to:

1. Evaluate informal playmaking.
2. Evaluate theatrical productions, films, and television plays.
3. Formulate and use criteria for judging theatre aesthetically.

Developmental Level Charts

The charts that follow provide a continuum of goals and objectives designed for the individual growth of the student at each of three levels of sophistication. Several activities are suggested which may help the student to achieve each objective listed under each level. The various levels of sophistication indicate beginning students at Level I, intermediate students at Level II, and advanced students at Level III. Age and maturity are often factors in a student's level of development in the theatre arts. (Beginning does not necessarily mean primary grades, nor does advanced necessarily signify upper division high school.)

Component One: Aesthetic Perception—Multisensory Integration

Goal I: To experience dramatic elements, actions, and characterizations

Objectives: The student will be able to:

1. Become perceptive and selective in observing and responding to the environment.
2. Use movement as the external expression of an internal idea, intention, or feeling.
3. Use the voice as an instrument for the expression of meaning and feeling, whether in speech or nonverbal sound.
4. Respond spontaneously and collaboratively to rapidly changing, unanticipated stimuli.

Concept/Content Area	Level I	Level II	Level III
Sensory and emotional awareness	Hold a real object and concentrate on all the senses.	Recall an experience, such as eating an ice cream cone, concentrating first on the sensory aspects and then on the actual feeling response.	Use sensory awareness in developing parts of improvisation and playmaking, using familiar story lines.
	Hold an imaginary object and react with all the senses.		
	React to imaginary sounds, eat imaginary food, touch imaginary objects of varying temperatures and textures, see imaginary objects, smell imaginary foods, react emotionally to imagined situations.		
Rhythm and movement	Jump, move arms, skip, hop, or run to rhythmic beat of music, handclapping, or music and rhythms created by other students.	Change directions in space—forward, backward, on diagonals, in circles and up or down.	Move abstractly (move as the color "blue" might move).
	Move as an object or animal or as different types of people.		

41

Concept/Content Area	Level I	Level II	Level III
Rhythm and movement (continued)	Change levels (melt like ice cream); change size or stance (move like a person who is fat, thin, short, or tall).	Represent moods in movement: sad, happy, and so forth.	Change the composition of space; become space.
			Demonstrate different emotional qualities.
		Play tug-of-war with an imaginary rope.	Experiment with different stage movement to gain dramatic effect.
			Collectively create complex movement patterns (the whole class creates a machine).
Pantomime	Be clothes hanging on a clothesline (the wind is blowing; the sun is shining; the rain is falling).	Manipulate and distinguish simple, imagined objects: pencil, baseball bat, iron, feather.	
		Discover how to communicate weight, size, volume, texture, and temperature.	
Oral communication	Reproduce sounds, such as those of birds, bears, lions, and so forth.	Recount personal experiences, tell stories, and the like.	Read scripts in which everything must be communicated solely through the voice.
	Reproduce machine sounds individually or with others; wind, thunder, rain, and so forth.		
	Combine sound with action.		

Component Two: Creative Expression

Goal I: To develop skills in storytelling, playmaking, and playwriting

Objectives: The student will be able to:
1. Retell and perform a story.
2. Perform an improvisation which is structured, played, evaluated, and replayed.
3. Write original scenes or plays from improvisations.
4. Create appropriate technical elements for such scenes or plays.

Concept/Content Area	Level I	Level II	Level III
Pantomime	Perform simple pantomimed activities: getting up in the morning, taking off clothes, walking a tightrope like an acrobat, and so forth.	Learn to extract the essential qualities of movement in the creation of stylized pantomime: catching butterfly, picking it up by the wings, holding it between the thumb and forefinger, and fluttering the other fingers as though they were butterfly wings, releasing the butterfly and following it with eyes.	
	Express characterization in simple situations: grandmother shopping and carrying packages		Develop story line with increasing details, precision, and sophistication. Use serious as well as comic subject matter.
	Use pantomime in story lines.		
Oral communication	Convey emotional qualities through speech in simple story dramatizations: a member of a baseball team engaged in an angry argument with the umpire; a frightened child lost in the woods who comes upon a stranger and asks for help.		
		Tell stories to others, attempting to bring dramatic impact to the spoken word.	
		Memorize scenes from plays which provide a wide range of character types requiring differing speech.	

Concept/Content Area	Level I	Level II	Level III
Oral communication (continued)		Pursue the four basic speech objectives: projection, articulation, variety, and timing.	Experiment with character voices and dialects.
		Communicate characterization through the voice: mean witch casting an evil spell; circus clown telling how sad it is to have such big feet.	
Improvisation	Improvise a story suggested by a box of props or costumes.	Improvise from ambiguous visual stimulus: a black cloth is spread over the floor.	Improvise scenes from short stories, poems, myths, and songs.
	Improvise familiar story lines.	Improvise a story based on perceptions of a picture shown. Movement and body language beginning from the structure of the picture or ending with that structure; e.g., *American Gothic*.	
			Improvise the sense of images in poetry. ("This is the way the world ends—not with a bang but a whimper.")
Playmaking	Retell and dramatize a story.	Participate in the development of story dramatizations.	Participate in the development of dramatizations based on stimuli other than stories: a painting, a property, a costume piece which may suggest a story which the class members can create and write from their own imaginations.
		Use the structural components of story improvisation: beginning, conflict, resolution, and ending.	
		Explore the basic components of the formal scene—characterization, conflict, motivation, setting—through a variety of improvisational exercises.	

Concept/Content Area	Level I	Level II	Level III
Playmaking (continued)			Use approximately the total environment (room, furniture, personal resources, other people, weather . .) to solve an improvisational problem.
			Perform increasingly sophisticated characterizations using voice, movement, and emotional involvement in interactions of increasing complexity built on the principles of support, trust, and cooperation.
Playwriting			Write plays individually or collaboratively from imagination and experiences.
			Perform outstanding original plays or theatrical events as part of the formal production program.
			Create original theatrical events which integrate live theatre with other media: photography, films, projections, lighting, music, original musical composition, and electronic sounds.
			Make decisions about scenic and property elements for original plays.
			Understand and manipulate level, space, and light in staging classroom dramatizations of original scenes or plays.

Goal II: To develop an awareness of the collaborative nature of playmaking

Objectives: The student will be able to:
1. Participate actively in the planning of a dramatization.
2. Perform group dramatizations.
3. Evaluate group effort in exploring and expressing ideas.

Concept/Content Area	Level I	Level II	Level III
Playmaking (in groups)	Develop a presentation of characters within short scenes.	Collaborate in the development of dialogue, movement, sequences, and motivations for conflict in dramatic presentations.	Apply dramatic components of exposition, complication, crisis, and resolution to group dramatization. Collaborate in evaluation of group presentations.

Goal III: To develop acting skills for theatrical performance

Objectives: The student will be able to:
1. Become proficient in basic acting skills.
2. Use basic elements of formal acting: characterization, conflict, motivation, and setting.
3. Acquire basic vocabulary related to formal acting.

Concept/Content Area	Level I	Level II	Level III
Formal acting techniques		Use basic acting vocabulary as scene work evolves through demonstration and experimentation. Use theatre terminology to express observations. Select and perform scenes from plays.	Develop proficiency in the basic acting skills, read acting text, observe teacher demonstrations, experiment in improvisation, and work with scripted material.

Concept/Content Area	Level I	Level II	Level III
Formal acting techniques (continued)			Audition for and perform roles in plays selected for the formal production program.
			Study verse drama and reader's theatre.
			Read and act in radio plays.
			Learn to use exercises to meet identifiable speech deficiencies. Meaningless and tiresome rote repetitions of rhymes and speech exercises are avoided. Use gibberish, foreign language gibberish, stage whisper, and vowel and consonant emphasis.
			Evaluate effectiveness of own acting patterns and make changes.
			Use improvisation to explore new characterization and movement: improvise scenes in the play which happen off stage and are merely inferred in the text; exchange roles; improvise dialogue for long and complex speeches and attempt to transfer the naturalness; improvise scenes which have lost their spontaneity.

Goal IV: To develop an awareness of the collaborative nature of theatre and the many skills needed to prepare a finished production

Objectives: The student will be able to:

1. Learn directing.
2. Learn stage managing.
3. Learn business managing; e.g., publicity, box office.
4. Learn design and technical elements of sets, lights, costumes, props, sound, and special effects.
5. Understand how other art forms, such as music, dance, visual arts, and literature, are used in drama/theatre.

Concept/Content Area	Level I	Level II	Level III
Directing	See how a play is put together through the telling and retelling of a simple story.		Learn through exploration and experimentation, augmented by teacher demonstration and explanation, basic principles of theatre direction: director's intent, script, interpretation, subtextual connotations, and style.
			Produce an original scene or play in any context and view the theatre concepts (intent, structure, effectiveness, and worth) from a directorial point of view.
			Make an increasing number of directorial decisions in classroom dramatizations.
			Choose a scene from theatre literature and imagine how it can be played. (Short stories are visualized and analyzed from the directorial point of view in class discussion.)
			Learn the structure of the dramatization (planning, playing, evaluating, replaying). Play a scene in several different ways: change intent; note change of structure as a result.
			Apply directorial principles to rehearsal of scene.
			Evaluate scenes to focus directly on the deliberate directorial efforts: intent and structure (composition, mood, tempo, and the like) and how effectiveness was achieved.

Concept/Content Area	Level I	Level II	Level III
Directing (continued)			Participate with and assist the teacher-director in producing the formal theatre production.
			Meet professional (or experienced) directors to share insights and experiences.
Managing		Learn basic safety concerns about the theatre: fire safety, scenery storage, backstage lighting, general backstage order, safe audience exits, and so forth.	
		Gain practical experience in managing aspects of the formal production. Class members assume responsibility for stage managing, house managing, and management of publicity and public relations work.	
		Students visit college, university, resident (professional and nonprofessional), and touring theatres to observe the management processes. Such exposure will alert interested students to career opportunities available in these areas.	
Designing and executing technical elements			
Costumes	A collection of costume pieces is readily available in the classroom to encourage students to experiment with costumes and for use as stimuli in developing characterization.		
	Students design costumes and create simple classroom effects.		
			Learn the basic principles of figure drawings in order to produce costume sketches.
			Learn the basic color principles in order to use color effectively in costume drawings and actual costumes.

Concept/Content Area	Level I	Level II	Level III
Designing and executing technical elements (continued):			
Costumes (continued)	Draw a mask to use as the beginning of "dress-up" roles.	Construct simple costume effects from an assortment of materials and crepe paper for hats, headdresses, and other such items.	Study the history of costumes from any texts available.
Settings		Acquire a working knowledge of basic technical terminology through demonstration and practical work. Create levels, stairs, and stage separations from a simple set of blocks, boxes, and cubes in various sizes. Design stage settings and properties. Relate designs to specific pieces of dramatic literature, or an original classroom-written play.	Learn the principles of scale and perspective drawing in order to plan stage settings. Learn the basics of architectural drawing to make floor plans. Create set pieces and properties from cardboard in miniature.
Lighting/sound		Make and operate simple classroom lighting and sound instruments. Utilize a simplified classroom lighting system to learn the fundamental purposes of stage lighting: visibility, naturalness, composition, and mood.	
Makeup		Experiment with the application of stage makeup.	

Concept/Content Area	Level I	Level II	Level III
Makeup (continued)			Study the kinds of application of stage makeup and their functions in aiding the actor to create convincing, realistic characters and to create imaginative, fanciful, nonrealistic characterizations.
Integration of the arts	Apply movement, visual, and aural effects to dramatic presentations.	Discuss how sensory and emotional stimuli, which are created in theatrical productions including radio, TV, and motion pictures, involve the other arts.	Analyze the use of artistic elements to create an aesthetically satisyfing performance.
			Design stage elements—setting, properties, lighting, costumes, and makeup—for the play's selected formal production program.
			Operate and maintain technical elements in the rehearsal and performance sequence of the formal production.
			Meet professional (or experienced) designers to share insights and experiences.
			Use techniques from other arts in the creation of dramatic presentations based on literature.

Component Three: Drama/Theatre Heritage—Historical and Cultural

Goal I: To develop a knowledge of and appreciation for drama/theatre heritage

Objectives: The student will be able to:

1. Recognize major themes, historical periods, and cultural backgrounds.
2. Recognize the importance of today's theatre as a means of understanding and appreciating cultural differences.

Concept/Content Area	Level I	Level II	Level III
Literature history	Acquire a knowledge of the theatre through storytelling, improvisation, and playmaking, using fairy tales, nursery rhymes, folklore, and myths.	Become aware of the length of theatrical history, together with a beginning awareness of the chronological order of theatre literature.	Study in depth the literature of the theatre in chronological order.
			Read and perform in scenes from plays from specific periods of theatre history.
			Study the history of the theatre in conjunction with the chronological order of the literature of the theatre.
		Read a variety of plays to expand knowledge of literature of the theatre.	
			Research the background, styles, period, and historical context of a play; obtain information about the physical theatre and the actor-audience relationship of the period.

Concept/Content Area	Level I	Level II	Level III
Literature history (continued)			Develop a series of scenes which represent a specific theme; for instance, women's changing role in society, as shown in *Antigone, The Doll's House,* and *For Colored Girls Who Commit Suicide When the Rainbow's Not Enough.*
Culture	Participate in simple theatrical activities from many cultures.	Where appropriate, present bilingual performances of scenes from plays in translation: Spanish-speaking students perform scenes from *Lope de Vega* in both Spanish and English. Analyze theatrical performances to discover general themes and experiences.	Analyze dramatic performance and character development as depicted by dramatists from different cultures and times. Evaluate social, psychological, and cultural effects of various theatrical media on own and other life-styles.

Component Four: Aesthetic Valuing

Goal I: To develop a system of aesthetic valuing of drama/theatre

Objectives: The students will be able to:

1. Evaluate informal playmaking.
2. Evaluate theatrical productions, films, and television plays.
3. Formulate and use criteria for judging theatre aesthetically.

Concept/Content Area	Level I	Level II	Level III
Viewing and reviewing	Learn to view a classroom dramatization guided by a focus of observation established by the teacher; then participate in constructive evaluations guided by the teacher.	Discuss classroom performances. Observe attentively and recall observations during the evaluation period. Understand the terminology of evaluation: intent, structure, effectiveness, and worth.	Participate in evaluation, noting effective elements and making suggestions for improvement. Apply the terminology of evaluation in drawing conclusions about the qualities of the work seen or read. Continue to take part in evaluations of more complexity and depth; the teacher continues to press the discipline of more precise and specific observation. Make deeper observations—character, theme, and meaning emerge in evaluation.

Concept/Content Area	Level I	Level II	Level III
Viewing and reviewing (continued)			Read and evaluate the literature of the theatre followed by formal productions where possible.
			Learn and use the terminology of theatre evaluation when reviewing exemplary theatre productions.
			Write critical evaluations for plays read or seen.
			Read selected works from the fields of literary criticism, dramatic criticism, and aesthetics, and apply their principles to classroom and formal productions.

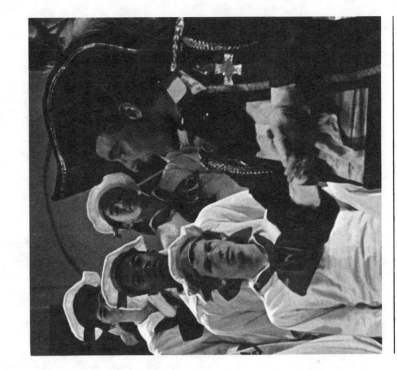

Program Development

Those developing a drama/theatre program need to consider certain essential aspects of such a program: curriculum planning, student performances, time and scheduling, teacher preparation, staff development, and community resources.

Curriculum Planning

The drama program on the elementary level should be geared to the development of each student's imagination, problem-solving ability, and communications skills. Once the basic techniques of drama have been learned, they can be incorporated into existing curricula. Storytelling, improvisation, and playmaking, for instance, can enhance and revitalize learning in the language arts and social studies. School administrators and the elementary school drama specialist should establish flexible scheduling blocks to ensure that regular, planned instruction in drama is provided for each elementary school child. If a performance aspect is added to the drama program, plays should be chosen for their educational worth and literary merit, and they should be meaningful for both actor and audience.

A drama/theatre curriculum on the secondary level must include courses which recognize drama as a

performing and technical art, an academic discipline, and an aesthetic experience. Drama/theatre teachers and school administrators should work together to develop the aims, objectives, and philosophy of each school's program. Schools should have courses in beginning, intermediate, and advanced theatre; play production; and stagecraft (including design and management). Larger schools should offer a wide diversity of course offerings, including, but not limited to, mass media (film, television), dramatic literature, and oral interpretation.

In addition to the development of drama/theatre courses and activities, criteria should be established for the careful selection of plays for production. The plays should be of educational worth and literary merit and must have meaning for the actors as well as for the students and community audience. Storytelling, mime, puppetry, maskmaking, television, and film are additional areas that can be included with great success in the drama/theatre curriculum. Each area offers unique opportunities for students to explore and develop the components of drama as well as to enhance their self-growth. Storytelling and puppetry lend themselves to all three levels of sophistication, while mime, television, and film are usually considered more advanced areas of specialization.

Storytelling is an art form through which a storyteller (any age) projects mental and emotional images to an audience using the spoken word, including sign language and gesture, carefully matching story content with audience needs and environment. The story sources reflect all literatures and cultures, fiction and nonfiction, for educational, historical, folkloric, entertainment, and therapeutic purposes.

A specialized form of movement, mime, is an idiom employing a traditional language of facial expression, gesture, and posture. It has its own costume and style of makeup and is often accompanied by music.

The art of transforming materials into a humanlike object, puppetry, has fast become one of the most popular forms of educational instruction in the elementary schools. Puppetry is an ideal instrument for aiding in language development and for helping a child to express feelings when he or she cannot confront another person directly.

Like puppetry, maskmaking transforms materials into a humanlike object, either one's actual face or a caricature of it. Theatres are using masks in diverse ways and are recognizing the making and the using of masks as two allied art forms.

Today's students are growing up in a media-oriented world. Their values, their ideas, and much of their learning have been shaped by television and film. Courses in television, film history, and production serve the purpose of getting students to think for themselves and to make constructive criticisms and judgments about the kinds of programs and films being presented constantly for their viewing and listening. Having students produce, direct, and act in their own original movie and television shows adds another dimension to theatre as an art form.

Student Performances

Students should also have the chance to work in reader's theatre, children's theatre, and improvisational or street theatre, depending on the needs and interests of the students and the community. In addition, an active theatre arts program would promote chamber theatre, one-act play festivals by student writers, "lunch-bag" or noontime theatre, festivals centering on the work of a major playwright, dance-mime programs, and multimedia concerts. Because performance is a unique and integral part of the theatre as art and

should be included at all levels with appropriate modifications, the following criteria relative to student performance in the elementary and secondary schools are proposed:

Elementary School Level

- Drama/theatre should be taught regularly as a separate subject and, when appropriate, should be used as a means for students to acquire subject matter competence.
- "Performance in process" for peers and "performance to share" with the community should be included at periodic levels at the teacher's discretion to meet the educational and artistic needs of the children.
- Drama/theatre is to be taught by a specialist in the field or by a classroom teacher adequately prepared to teach drama as an art and to use it as a teaching process.

Secondary School Level

- Drama/theatre classes are an integral part of the secondary school curriculum.
- Theatre performance in the "nonprofessional production" mode should be an extension of training in the drama/theatre classroom.
- The quality of performance must provide a positive aesthetic

experience for the players and audience.

- Any student participating in a drama/theatre program who demonstrates a commitment to the art and who accepts the discipline required of a performer should be given opportunities to perform.
- The qualified teacher of drama/theatre should have the final word in determining performance readiness.

Time and Scheduling

The scope of a drama/theatre program varies from school to school. Such factors as school size, geographical location, budget limitations, and type of community often act as determinants. Drama should be taught at the elementary level a minimum of 200 minutes every ten days, and secondary school students should be required to take at least one year of theatre at both the junior and senior high school level.

Teacher Preparation

To maximize the value and impact of drama/theatre for all California schoolchildren, educators must reexamine preservice and in-service teacher training programs. Providing additional training for teachers currently in the field as well as training new teachers for drama/theatre is necessary if the benefits of the program are to be made available to young people. The task remains to establish new programs for the preparation of teachers and to develop instructional materials to facilitate new teaching techniques.

Staff Development/Drama Theatre Specialists

Since the current multiple-subjects credential requirements do not include university or college drama courses, most elementary school teachers must depend on in-service workshops, university summer courses in child

drama, and the sharing of techniques with other teachers. Until training in drama becomes mandatory for all who seek the multiple-subjects credential, school administrators should make every effort to employ a drama specialist who can oversee and direct instruction, curriculum, and performing aspects of the drama program. The elementary school drama specialist would be responsible for conducting in-service training programs as well as serving as director/producer for those schools desiring children's theatre productions. The specialist could enlist the aid of storytellers, puppeteers, mime artists, artists-in-residence, and professional and school touring groups whose performances demonstrate a sense of creative play.

Because theatre is both an academic discipline and a performing art, specialists in the theatre arts are essential in secondary schools. Drama/theatre specialists at the secondary level should not only possess an academic major in theatre, but they should also be practitioners of the art; e.g., a performer, director, or designer. Although the size of the school, the nature of the community, and the availability of facilities and budget must be considered in the implementation of a quality secondary school theatre program, at least two qualified staff members (either on a full or partial assignment) should be employed by each school:

- *A teacher-director* with a theatre major who will teach subject matter and basic theatre skills, direct theatre productions, and coordinate supporting personnel (designer-technician, music instructor, dance instructor, and so forth)
- *A designer-technician* with a background in architecture, scenery, costume, lighting, and design for the theatre who will teach stagecraft and set and costume design and direct all technical aspects of theatrical productions

In school districts which contain several secondary schools, two specialists to supervise and coordinate the theatre program should be employed:

- *A supervisor of theatre* who will be responsible for overseeing instruction and curriculum; advising administrators concerning employment of teacher-directors; coordinating the selection and distribution of texts, classroom materials, and audiovisual teaching aids; coordinating production schedules throughout the district; and coordinating in-service training projects

- *A supervisor of technical theatre* who will oversee construction and/or improvement of educational housing for the performing arts; advise administrators concerning the employment and assignment of designer-technicians; coordinate the purchasing and distribution of theatrical equipment; coordinate the storage and distribution of reusable theatrical materials: sets, props, furniture, and costumes; and assist the theatre supervisor with in-service training projects

Community Resources

Other resources beneficial to the drama/theatre program are professional storytellers, puppeteers, mime artists, artists-in-residence, and professional and school touring groups. A theatre program can benefit from a boosters' or parents' club and by the opportunity to use certain community buildings as performing spaces. In addition, field trips to professional and community theatre groups and festivals and contests will aid students' critical assessment abilities as well as set new standards for their own performances. Most advanced students may get career ideas from a backstage tour or a visit to an agent's office.

Students with Special Needs

The diversity of theatre arts activities provides opportunities for the involvement of all students, regardless of experience, cultural background, or disabling conditions. Students alternate as creators, observers, and evaluators, developing an understanding and appreciation of the abilities and efforts of others.

Gifted and Talented Students

Gifted students especially need the enrichment and stimulation that come from a drama/theatre program. Because of the experiential nature of drama/theatre, gifted or talented students will automatically be challenged to expand their creative and intellectual talents. Traditionally, teaching gifted students has meant more individualized instruction, cluster grouping, less teacher lecture, and more student direction and participation. The typical drama/theatre classroom already provides such requirements. Additionally, the inevitable variety found in the heterogeneous drama classroom provides a rich resource of life-styles, attitudes, and cultural distinctions which provide creative challenges, in-depth experiences, and leadership opportunities for the gifted student.

Students in Special Education

Students with special education needs, defined as those who have either emotional, physical, intellectual, or educational problems in coping with their environment, benefit from drama/theatre experiences. Drama/theatre offers these students the opportunity to participate in activities which help to develop their strengths, minimize their weaknesses, and foster good social relationships based on interaction with others. The activities help to build a positive self-image, since students contribute their ideas and share in the

drama/theatre activities required to bring others' ideas to life.

A sensitive teacher will find that most of the activities suggested in this chapter may be adapted for the special education student within the limitations of the child's ability. The classroom teacher is not a professional therapist, but by knowing the special students in the class—their problems and needs—the teacher may apply the techniques of drama/theatre to effect growth, self-expression, and social interaction.

Multicultural Education

The drama/theatre experience is an ideal instrument for developing and enriching bilingual and multicultural programs, because drama allows the student to experience feelings, sensations, and ideas first hand—to see through the eyes of another. Students from different ethnic groups have an opportunity to share with others their cultural expression, personal ethics, and social goals.

Theatre arts expand cultural awareness. The study of the great dramatic masterpieces, a prerequisite for bringing them to life on the stage, creates an appreciation and appetite for good literature. The study of theatre history shows universality as well as the influences of one cultural style on another.

Knowledge of the artistic accomplishments of the world's great cultures enables students to grasp the relevance of the arts in the structure of society. The rich heritage of the theatrical tradition derives from the contributions of multiethnic groups. Recognition of national and cultural differences and commonalities reveals the universalities of human emotions and experiences.

Careers in Drama/Theatre

The goal of drama/theatre teachers in the public schools is not to train students for acting careers. Through work in drama, students will acquire poise, self-confidence, and skills in self-expression and speaking that will be useful in any career.

In addition, theatre arts develop physical skills. Students come to appreciate the dignity of human labor, because the theatre demands a great amount of physical labor. They perfect techniques for handling lumber, paint, cloth, tools, and electrical equipment. They launder clothing, upholster furniture, sell tickets, and work within budgets.

Theatre arts contribute to vocational education. Training and practical experience in a diversity of skills provide a comprehensive background for students seeking careers in community and professional theatre, dance, television, and the motion picture industry. Examples of the types of career opportunities available in the television and film industries (exclusive of the more obvious actor, director, writer, producer) are floor manager, projectionist, cinematographer, camera operator, switcher, lighting designer, makeup designer, costumer, scene designer, and graphic artist.

Evaluation of Student Progress

Since the drama/theatre experience is based on personal growth, self-evaluation is a natural result of the process. Written and verbal evaluation by both student and teacher are, therefore, more relevant to the students and their progress than a letter grade. As the teachers evaluate students' work in class, they establish qualitative evaluation in the form of questions (What? Why? What other way? and How else?) rather than right or wrong, good or bad. This method of evaluation encourages rather than discourages the student and provides new insights and directions for achievement. The teacher must choose the appropriate criteria by which each specific area of the student's growth will be measured.

Environment, Materials, and Equipment

Elementary school drama programs require flexible classroom playing areas or a large, open playing space. A multipurpose room is desirable for playmaking activities that result in a performance situation. A storage area in classrooms (cabinets, shelves, and so forth) for props, costumes, or curriculum materials is also required. For those schools which have a children's theatre component (theatre by children for children), a performance space similar to that required by the secondary schools is desirable.

The secondary school theatre program requirement is unique in that the type of space is more important than its size. Two areas must be provided: (1) a classroom and resource center; and (2) a theatre or auditorium. The drama classroom should be a large room which has movable furniture, affords a rehearsal space equivalent to that of the stage, and can accommodate a small audience for laboratory production. (An ideal requirement would include smaller rehearsal rooms for acting exercises and short scenes.) The resource center would contain the following:

- Books (plays, scenes, monologues, theatre history, biography, and technology)
- Theatre magazines (*Theatre Crafts, Dramatics, American Film*)
- Recordings (plays, dialects, poetry)
- Visuals (slides, prints, models)

The theatre or auditorium should be a facility designed for presentation of plays and musicals as opposed to that designed for symphony concerts, assemblies, or motion pictures. The following represents an "ideal" situation:

- Audience area—raked floor, capacity 200—700 seats
- Stage area—proscenium arch opening 18 by 35 feet (5.4 by 10.5 metres); depth 35 feet (10.5 metres); offstage area—an equal number of square feet or metres, one-half on each side of the stage area
- Equipment—switchboard, lighting instruments, sound system (amplifier, speakers, microphones, turntable, tape deck), videotape recorder
- Dressing rooms, equipped with toilets, showers, and makeup rooms for the actors
- Audience restrooms

Since the ideal theatre or auditorium is not always available, the following could be substituted:

- A flat space at least 20 by 40 feet (6 by 12 metres) for rehearsals and/or construction
- A performance space of about the same size, with extra space for audience seating
- Good acoustics
- Restrooms for the audience, away from the backstage areas
- Backstage area with rooms in which actors can change into costumes and apply makeup; restrooms with mirrors; storage space which can be locked (for costumes and makeup)
- Sound system: A cassette or reel-to-reel tape recorder, turntable, amplifier, two speakers, microphone, and lockable storage for these items (for Levels II and III)
- Lighting equipment: Basics for a 20 by 40 feet (6 by 12 metres) area should include: 16 Fresnel-type instruments or their equivalent in small ellipsoidal instruments (500—750 watts), control system (dimmers for lights), extra lamps for instruments (one for every two instruments), cable to patch instruments into lighting control system, and color media for lighting instruments

The following service areas must be available for both types of theatre facilities:

1. Construction area, which includes:
   Tools and tool crib (one set of tools for every four students), storage cabinets which can be locked

2. Storage area for the following items:
   Furniture
   Costumes
   Properties
   Set pieces
   Draperies, drops, cycloramas
   Makeup

3. Costume construction area, which includes:

Sewing machine
Iron and ironing board
Storage space for sewing and designing tools

Conclusion to Chapter 3

One of the major purposes of drama/theatre in today's world is to help the student develop the "self." Through participation in drama/theatre activities, students learn to discover, express, and accept themselves.

We must no longer think of drama/theatre simply as Shakespeare, Shaw, or a specific play. We must think of it as the opportunities it affords students to find the greatness in this life and to give it meaning.

Chapter 4

Music

Music plays an *essential* role in the education of all students. Music is a unique language for expression.

Music—

- Expresses spiritual and emotional values that are both personal and universal
- Expands the creative capabilities of each person
- Integrates and harmonizes the mind and body
- Promotes a sense of well-being
- Contributes to increased learning capacities in diverse subject areas

Music is intellectually stimulating and challenging:

Music is a fine art. It is also a discipline. It both expresses and arouses feelings that are emotionally compelling. It also challenges the mind. *What* it communicates is felt. *How* it communicates must be understood. Few subjects in the curriculum can match music in the simultaneous interactive involvement of both the emotions and the intellect.[1]

Music is part of every culture, and its place in each culture is significant.

The intent of the music education chapter of the framework is to maintain, extend, and build upon ideas that were presented in the 1971 California music framework. That publication was "based on the idea that music education should . . . be aesthetic education." Further, it was stated that "the general purpose of music education is to develop aesthetic sensitivity to music in children, that is, to heighten the quality and impact of their musical experiences."[2]

---

[1]William C. Hartshorn, "The Study of Music as an Academic Discipline." A paper presented at the opening session of the Music Educators National Conference, 1962.

[2]*Music Framework for California Public Schools: Kindergarten Through Grade Twelve.* Sacramento: California State Department of Education, 1971. pp. 3-4.

Other guidelines were taken from the report on the Tanglewood Symposium, which was held in the summer of 1967, wherein it was pointed out that "music serves best when its integrity as an art is maintained." The report also stated that "the music teachers' responsibility is to become increasingly aware of the aesthetic needs not only of all their students but also of the entire community in which they serve."[3]

The music chapter is designed as a framework for a music curriculum at all levels. For this reason certain sections are not designated solely for elementary or secondary levels. The information is presented as a continuum organized into developmental levels which the learner may enter at any age. It remains for each district and each teacher to develop specific activities which are appropriate at a given grade.

One of the themes which emerged from the 1978-79 Ann Arbor Symposium reinforces this manner of organizing information. It states, "You are always building from structures that are already there, and, as developmental research suggests, these can emerge at different stages .... Don't jump to the conclusion that sequencing must follow a precise chronology .... There are probably periods when learning takes place more easily or when people go farther and faster, but ... it is never too late."[4]

Terms in Music

Characteristic objectives—Objective statements which describe basic musical behaviors that students need to develop to achieve a specific goal

Components—Organizers for the goals, objectives, and content

Illustrative activities—Sample activities intended to serve as examples to guide developers of state, individual school, or district courses of study, continuums, and instructional guides

Selected concepts—A listing of fundamental understanding basic to musical growth

Components and Goals in Music Education

The four components adopted in this *Visual and Performing Arts Framework*—aesthetic perception, creative expression, music heritage, both historical and cultural, and aesthetic valuing—are employed here as a means of organizing goals, objectives, and content. Under each of the components, goals are detailed and content is defined by means of a list of suggested concepts which students should develop. The charts, which begin on page 74, relate components, goals and objectives, and content; and they also present illustrative examples of appropriate activities.

Component One: Aesthetic Perception—Perceptual and Conceptual Development

The goals of music education that relate primarily to the perception component are:

- To develop sensitivity to the expressive qualities of music
- To increase aural awareness
- To encourage musical responsiveness, involvement, and discrimination
- To promote understanding of the nature and structure of music

The perception of sound is the first step in musical learning. The learner then develops concepts about music

---

[3]Louis G. Wersen and others. "Tanglewood, A Charge to Music Education," in *The Tanglewood Symposium, Music in American Society.* Washington, D.C.: Music Educators National Conference, n.d., pp. 139-40.

[4]Judith Murphy, "Conflict, Consensus, and Communication," *Music Educators Journal,* Vol. 66 (March, 1980), 5—31.

based on these various perceptions. The ongoing process involves discriminating and comparing, generalizing, organizing sounds, and, ultimately, making applications from these developing concepts to new encounters in musical experiences.

Because of this intimate relationship of initial perception and the growth of understanding, the content suggested for the perception component goes beyond the first step of perceiving to include conceptual development. The content material is organized here in three areas: sound, the elements of music, and notation.

Sound

Educators should provide students with the bases for understanding the nature of sound. The scientific and mathematical relationships of sound and the tonal possibilities available for use in making music have historically been a source of wonder for humanity and a challenge for the musician.

Some of the concepts that may be developed are:

- Sound is produced in diverse ways and can be modified.
- The human voice and musical instruments are unique generators of sound.
- Sound has certain characteristics which are variable.
- Sound can be used for special effects.
- Sound can produce psychological effects.
- Tonal and rhythmic relationships have mathematical bases.

Elements of Music

Musical sound may be thought of as sound that is organized. The elements of music are those aspects of sound around which this organization takes place. Students must understand the relationships among these elements: pitch, rhythm, harmony, form, texture, tempo, dynamics, and timbre.

Concepts of Pitch:

- Pitches may be high or low, or they may repeat.
- Melody is created when pitches and silences occur successively.
- A progression of pitches creates a melodic contour.
- Scales are built on pitches organized with particular tonal relationships.
- Melodic meaning is affected by range, register, length of melodic groupings, and size of intervals.
- Many melodies have tonal centers which serve as points of aural focus.

Concepts of Rhythm:

- Musical sound is measured by units of time. These pulses or beats can be organized in sets (meter) which move in twos or threes or multiples and combinations thereof.
- Longer and shorter tones can be grouped in patterns which are repeated.

- Rhythmic patterns can contribute to the feel of an underlying pulse but are distinguished from the pulse.

Concepts of Harmony:

- When two or more tones are heard simultaneously, harmony is created.
- Three or more tones sounded simultaneously form a *chord*.
- Chords can be modified by altering some of their tones and by adding more tones.

Concepts of Form:

- The ways in which the elements of music interact with one another contribute to the design of the music.
- Phrases or sections can be identical or different according to the repetition or variation of the elements.
- Repetition of patterns, phrases, or sections creates unity in a musical composition.
- Contrasting phrases or sections provide variety in a musical composition.

Concepts of Texture:

- The total sound of a piece of music may have varying textures: thick, thin, opaque, transparent, and so forth.

- Individual melodic and rhythmic motifs may have textures, such as legato and staccato.

Concepts of Tempo:

- The rate of speed of a composition or section is called tempo.
- Tempo affects the character of the music.
- Some compositions have sections that are slower or faster than others to provide contrast and variety.
- Sensitivity to tempo adds to the expressiveness of a performance.

Concepts of Dynamics:

- *Dynamics* refers to the comparative loudness and softness of music.
- The expressive effect of music is changed when the dynamics are changed significantly.
- Different musical terms are used for the various dynamic levels in music.
- Sensitivity to dynamics adds to the expressiveness of a performance.

Concepts of Timbre:

- The human voice can produce different tonal qualities.
- Families of orchestral instruments have characteristic sounds.
- Each orchestral instrument has a characteristic sound (timbre).
- The instruments of different cultures produce characteristic musical sounds which are unique to these cultures.

Notation

The reference to notation under this component has to do with the visual perceptions of sound. Notation will reappear under Component Two as a skill in reading and writing.

Suggested concepts are:

- Music may be recorded in written form.
- Music may be notated with a variety of symbol systems.

Component Two: Creative Expression—Musical Skills Development

Involvement in musical expression requires that the participants develop technical skills. The material under the creative expression component, therefore, will be presented under the heading of *skills,* rather than *concepts.* Interaction among the various musical concepts and skills is essential. Perception of sound is central. As students develop skills in performing, creating, and analyzing, concurrent conceptual development provides the basis for students' *complete* understanding.

The goal of music education that relates to this component is to develop necessary skills so that students may function as capable and intelligent performers, creators, and consumers of music

The goals of music education that relate to this component are:

- To become sensitive to the expressive qualities of musical sounds
- To develop musical responsiveness, involvement, and discrimination
- To develop skills necessary to become capable and intelligent performers, creators, and consumers of music

Skills essential to growth in musicality are:

1. The auditory skill, or the skill of attentive listening, which is the basic and indispensable activity in music education. The development of aural acuity, a prerequisite to musical growth, is of extreme importance to students in all of their learning activities. Through listening, students develop sensitivity to the quality of musical sounds. They must learn to listen not only with the outer ear but also with the inner ear of the mind, so that they become able to "think" tone; e.g., to hear a melody in the mind when no sound is actually being produced.

Any discussion of listening must take into account not only the listener as a perceiver but also the nature of music itself. Unlike the materials of other arts, which we can see and touch as objects that remain conveniently static in space for our examination, a musical tone moves in time. The implications of this fact are far reaching, for if the listener is to understand a piece of music, that music must be retained in the mind.

The development of listening skills, therefore, is basic to a person's success in all the activities that contribute to one's musical development.

2. Translative skills or skills of reading and writing music:

Students' experiences with the sound of music must precede their contact with visual symbols. The symbols of musical notation take on meaning for children when these symbols represent tonal or rhythmic groupings they have already sung, heard, or played. The first symbols a child may see will probably convey only general meaning, such as the overall contour of a melody, and, in many cases, these symbols may have no relation to the staff. As children's musical experiences continue, they come to understand notational symbols that convey more precise musical meaning, and notes on a staff begin to be understood as indicating the pitch and rhythm of the music they have previously experienced by ear.

The purposes of visual experiences with musical notation are to help children see what they hear and hear what they see.

Drill on elements of staff notation, such as key signatures, the names of isolated notes and intervals, meter signatures, and the like, will not in itself promote growth in music reading; however, these factors should be taught as the need arises in singing and playing activities. Improvement in reading music will occur only when the children concentrate on the notation itself as they hear or produce musical sounds and when they have developed the aural acuity to translate the visual symbols.

3. Creative skills, which include producing both improvised and written music:

A correlative of prime importance to listening attentively, to performing music, and to reading music is creating music, whose development should parallel other musical activities. Student improvisation and composing must be cultivated continually.

As student growth continues in musical skills and understandings, students' modes of expression in composition should also develop more sophistication. Students should be encouraged to explore and develop musical concepts through their own creative efforts and to apply the results of their explorations to their original compositions.

4. Performance skills, which include singing, playing of instruments, body movement, and conducting:

a. Singing

The singing voice is part of the individual and, as such, provides an intimate musical experience. Many positive experiences through singing contribute greatly to an individual's musical growth as well as vocal development.

Vocal material should be carefully selected in relation to the physical development of students' voices. This approach is particularly important during the children's beginning stages of singing and at upper elementary and junior high school levels when some students' voices begin to change.

Understanding the structure of a song, its melodic contour, intervallic relationships, rhythmic character, chordal structure, harmonic relationships, style, form, and expressive elements contributes to growth in an individual's interpretive skill. Such analysis is also essential to the process of developing concepts of the elements of music and of understanding their interrelationships. Musical concepts grow out of perceptual experiences with

music, and singing is an activity that can provide opportunities for such experiences if the singers truly listen as they sing.

b. Playing Instruments

The use of instruments in the promotion of musical learning is of genuine value. Classroom music experiences involving simple percussion and tonal instruments can be used as a means of helping students develop concepts of sound, musical sound, pitch, rhythm, dynamics, tempo, and timbre.

Skills in reading notation can be enhanced through the playing of simple wind instruments, such as the tonette, flutophone, songflute, and recorder. In addition, melody instruments can be used to accompany singing to produce effects of harmony.

Class instruction in the playing of wind, string, and percussion instruments should be available to students. In addition, when students have reached a degree of proficiency that qualifies them to play in orchestral and band ensembles, the school should provide them with the opportunity to do so.

c. Body Movement

Movement to music is much more than a means of relaxation and recreation; it is a discipline as well. At all levels of instruction, the aim should be to increase the students' acuity of perception by exploring all the elements of music through movement. A wide range of music and modes of presentation should be used so that students may experience these elements effectively.

d. Conducting

Interpreting music through conducting is another avenue of expression. Even young children can begin experiencing the elements of music through conducting; e.g., indicating changes of dynamics, tempo, and pitch for speech chants. Sensitivity to the expressive qualities of music is refined as the students mature in their conducting skills.

5. Skill in musical analysis, a process of inquiry, in which the student compares and differentiates, then verbalizes and generalizes the experience

The development of skills in this area begins during the early school years and is nurtured and refined throughout the student's educational life. Beginning with the discrimination of concepts of sound, vocabulary development (musical terms), and identification of various aspects of musical compositions, students become increasingly sophisticated as they

progress. During the ensuing years they develop proficiencies which allow them to listen to music with increased understanding, analyze and discuss music using the appropriate vocabulary, and criticize their own works as well as the works of fellow students. Older students who have had the benefit of continual, sequential experiences and instruction in music can knowledgeably listen to and discuss music. They develop the ability to encounter unfamiliar musical experiences and new musical phenomena and make judgments based upon their own analytical skills.

Component Three: Music Heritage—Historical and Cultural

A comprehensive program of instruction will foster the simultaneous development of understanding and skills within the historical/cultural context. The goal of this component of the program is:

To develop awareness and understanding of the styles, idioms, performance media, and purposes of musics that are part of our multicultural heritage

The study of the musics of the world, and of historical periods and styles, will reveal the relationships between music and the lives of people. Students' perspectives will be deepened as they comprehend these relationships. As historical and cultural studies are interwoven in the curriculum, certain concepts will emerge, such as:

- Music is a part of living and is related to historical and social movement; people use music to communicate and to express feelings, to lighten labors, to tell about their world, and to satisfy emotional needs.
- Music has a use in therapy with power to affect human behavior.
- Social influences affect choices in music.

- Musical instruments as they exist today have evolved from very simple and basic beginnings.
- People use the material of their environment to create instruments.
- Music has its own major forms, stylistic periods, and cultural characteristics.

Component Four: Aesthetic Valuing

As students expand their musical knowledge, as they understand the various uses of music, and as they use this information while hearing, performing, and creating music, they begin to make choices from a variety of aesthetic options. As they draw from these numerous options, the students need to have a set of values upon which to base their judgments. These values cannot be taught as if they were concepts or skills. They *can* be acquired in the individual through the attainment of other goals and objectives of the music curriculum.

Aesthetic sensitivity extends beyond the acquisition of knowledge and skills. It can be viewed as the realization that a wide range of values does exist in the arts. In the same way musicality involves the placing of value on the comprehension of beauty and the expression of feeling in music. For this reason aesthetic experiences with music should be provided daily, keeping students in touch with the beauty of sound and great works of art.

The goal of this component of the program is: to provide a sound basis of musical experience which students can use in making intelligent judgments of musical value.

Some concepts in aesthetic valuing are:

- Music is a unique medium for human expression.
- Knowledge about music can increase one's ability to choose alternatives that are meaningful to the individual.

- The ability to make aesthetic judgments will heighten the pleasure that can be found in music.

Developmental Level Charts

As described in Chapter 1, the charts that follow relate the components, the goals and objectives, and the content areas of music education. The illustrative activities described on these levels indicate only a few of the steps through which the objectives, and thereby the goals, can be accomplished. The activities are intended to be applicable to students of all ages. The activities at Level I, for instance, are appropriate for students who are beginning their study of music, whether they be preschoolers or collegians.

Component One: Aesthetic Perception—Perceptual and Conceptual Development

Goals

1. To develop sensitivity to the expressive qualities of music
2. To increase aural awareness
3. To encourage musical responsiveness, involvement, and discrimination
4. To promote understanding of the nature and structure of music

Objectives: Students will:

1. Demonstrate an understanding of how sound is generated and modified.
2. Demonstrate an understanding of the elements of music.
3. Demonstrate an understanding of the structure (form and design) in music.
4. Demonstrate understandings which will lead to the effective use of written notation.

Concept Area	Developmental Level I	Developmental Level II	Developmental Level III
Sound			
Sound generation	Experiment with various ways of making sound.	Identify the mode of vibration in a variety of sound sources; e.g., voice, found objects, instruments.	Cagetorize sounds by the manner in which they are produced.
Sound modification	Explore various means by which sounds can be changed.	Identify the sound sources by the manner in which their sounds are changed or modified.	Analyze the factors which can induce changes in sound.
Musical elements			
Pitch	Demonstrate pitch differences through moving, playing, or singing.	Identify relative or absolute pitch relationships by syllables, numbers, or hand signs.	Independently produce and identify intervals and melodies.
Rhythm	Imitate rhythm patterns accurately.	Identify beat and divisions of the beat.	Differentiate among the rhythmic characteristics in various works of music.

Concept Area	Developmental Level I	Developmental Level II	Developmental Level III
Harmony	Combine speech patterns in canon and with ostinati.	Identify polyphonic, homophonic, and monophonic structures.	Analyze harmonic structure aurally.
Form	Demonstrate like and unlike phrases visually, aurally, and kinesthetically.	Identify and label simple musical forms.	Analyze structure and form as music is being performed, created, or experienced.
Texture	Recognize the differences in texture in selected examples of music.	Demonstrate, in movement or visual representation, the texture of sound within a composition.	Identify and label examples of texture as they occur; i.e., homophonic, polyphonic, and monophonic.
Tempo and dynamics	Demonstrate variations of fast and slow and loud and soft through movement, playing, or singing.	Use appropriate terms for identifying tempo and dynamics.	Analyze how composers and performers use tempo and dynamics.
Timbre	Recognize differences in tone color.	Label sounds produced by various types of instruments, voices, and other sources.	Analyze how composers and performers have produced particular qualities of sound.
Notation symbols	Move to draw melodic contour of simple melodies.	Match the melodic contour which is heard with a written version of that example.	Analyze different ways in which music may be recorded in written form.

Component Two: Creative Expression—Musical Skills Development

Goals

1. To become sensitive to the expressive qualities of musical sounds
2. To develop musical responsiveness, involvement, and discrimination
3. To develop skills necessary to become capable and intelligent performers, creators, and consumers of music

Objectives: Students will:

1. Listen and respond to music accurately and intellectually.
2. Perform music using a variety of sound sources.
3. Communicate musical ideas effectively through the use of notation.
4. Demonstrate ability to develop and communicate original musical ideas.

Skills	Level I	Level II	Level III
Singing	Sing melodies with increasing accuracy of pitch and rhythm.	Sing rounds, descants, and songs in two or more parts.	Sing from more complex vocal literature, using sophisticated techniques.
	Participate in group singing; e.g., assembly sings.	Perform alone as well as in a group.	Participate in choral groups.
Playing	Play simple ostinatos and bourdons on tonal instruments, such as melody bells, resonator bells, glockenspiels, xylophones, and the like.	Play simple melodies on tonal instruments.	Perform alone as well as in a group.
	Strum the autoharp with the pulse of the music in accompanying songs.	Play simple chordal accompaniments on instruments, such as the autoharp, guitar, or resonator bells.	Play complex chordal accompaniments on instruments, such as the guitar, piano, and other keyboard instruments.
	Play simple percussion instruments with accurate rhythm and appropriate dynamics as they accompany songs, chants, or recorded instrumental compositions.	Play simple melodies on tonal instruments.	Perform alone as well as in a group.
			Participate in band, orchestra, and/or other instrumental performing groups.

Skills	Level I	Level II	Level III
Moving	Demonstrate the pulse of music with bodily movement.	Use the body to represent rhythm structures.	Conduct in duple or triple meter.
	Demonstrate the rhythm of a melody in movement.	Use the body to represent melodic contour.	Express thematic development with movement ideas.
	Illustrate like and unlike phrases through movement.	Create dance patterns to illustrate form.	Illustrate polyphonic structure through movement.
Reading and writing	Use line notation and hand signs with accuracy. Write and read own symbols for sound.	Accurately interpret standard notation, using syllables, numbers, and/or hand signs.	Interpret and perform written music accurately.
Creating	Improvise simple tunes and rhythms, using the voice, body, or musical instruments.	Improvise more complex melodies and rhythmic patterns, using appropriate sound sources.	Arrange original musical compositions for chosen performance media; e.g., choral, orchestral, ballet.
	Create simple original melodic patterns.	Create original compositions.	Record ideas using standard or original notation.
Listening	Identify and differentiate accurately among the various musical characteristics.	Hear and identify larger components within the elements, structure, and styles of music.	Identify the more subtle details within the elements, structure, and styles of music.

Component Three: Music Heritage—Historical and Cultural

Goal: To develop awareness and understanding of the styles, idioms, performance media, and purposes of musics that are part of our multicultural heritage

Objectives: Students will:

1. Identify and become familiar with the extent of their own musical heritage.
2. Identify some of the expressive elements in the music of different cultures and ethnic groups.
3. Describe some of the social and historical situations which influenced the composition, style, selection, and performance of music.

Content Area	Level I	Level II	Level III
Personal heritage	Participate in playing and hearing music of their own ethnic and cultural group, as well as that of other students.	Develop time lines highlighting events in their individual musical heritage.	Compare their own individual music heritages with those of others.
Cultural musical contributions	Listen to music from many cultures.	Understand how composers have drawn inspiration from music of regional and national origins.	Compare the similarities and differences in styles, performance media, and tone colors in various cultures.
	Listen to music of various cultures.	Explore the qualities of sound that are expressive of different cultures.	Analyze how the distinctive sounds of music, such as jazz and folk, are determined by the performance media.
Social and historical influences	Discuss various purposes of music; e.g., lullabies, marches, dirges.	Analyze how the purpose of music affects the character of music.	Analyze how the social and environmental influences of a cultural or ethnic group shape the character of the music.
	Experience music designed for various purposes.	Recognize the different functions of music and how the function dictates the style and form.	Analyze how music can be used to affect emotions.

Component Four: Aesthetic Valuing

Goal: To provide a sound basis of musical experience which can be used in making intelligent judgments of musical value

Objectives: Students will:

1. Demonstrate an understanding of the value and role of music in the lives of individuals and cultures.
2. Demonstrate an understanding of how the purpose and function of music in a particular situation have influenced composition, selection, and performance.
3. Demonstrate an understanding of the ways in which the elements of music have been combined to produce characteristic styles and forms.

Concept/Content Area	Level I	Level II	Level III
Cultural background	Recognize that world music is derived from diverse backgrounds.	Differentiate between cultural and historical sources that determine form and style.	Choose, for a specific purpose, from a variety of musical styles and support choices.
Judgment	Willingly listen to recorded music and attend live concerts.	Begin to develop an appreciation for certain selections, performers, and composers. Begin to use one's own criteria for making these selections.	Rationalize and defend musical preferences.
Function	Recognize the appropriateness of different forms of music for different occasions.	Categorize forms of music as to function and purpose.	Rationalize and defend appropriate choices of music according to function.
Musical structure and elements	Distinguish between the elements of music.	Develop criteria that will aid in increasing the sensitivity of students to the elements of music as they perform, create, and listen to music.	Analyze musical elements for one's own purpose as a listener, performer, or composer.

Program Development

Those developing a music education program need to consider certain essential aspects of such a program: curriculum planning, suggested class offerings, student performance in public, schedules for activities, teacher preparation, music coordinators, music specialists, staff development, community resources, live performances, and artists-in-schools programs.

Curriculum Planning

An effective program of music education provides instruction for students from the preschool years through high school. Concern for a well-planned music curriculum should be jointly shared by teachers, principals, parents, and other members of the school community. All have a unique contribution to make. Most significantly, music and curriculum coordinators should become aware of and responsive to these concerns as they assume the task of developing music curriculum. Such planning must go full circle, however, and curriculum developers must be responsible not only for organizing the instructional program but also for interpreting its broader goals and objectives to the teaching staff, school and district administrators, parents, and the community at large. The anticipated result would be the support of the entire music program (K—12) so that students would be assured of having a sequence of instruction which provides the opportunities and experiences that permit them to participate and progress to their fullest potential.

In considering today's challenges, music curriculum developers need to examine alternative avenues for planning, rather than relying solely on "tried and true" models and simple reforms of past plans. Program planners can profit from the advice of Violet Allain, who suggests that individuals "learn to appreciate change and consider the consequence of a range of alternatives."[5]

Schools should examine their music curriculum on a regular basis to determine its continued effectiveness. At the same time music educators are urged, more than ever, to embrace the challenge espoused by the Music Educators National Conference "to return to their original role—to accept as their first responsibility the time-honored objective of music for every child."[6]

Guidelines for maintaining and expanding music education programs should include:

- A philosophy and well-defined goals
- A curriculum which begins on the preschool level and extends through high school
- Access to this curriculum by all students
- A plan for systematic evaluation

Experiences should be broad-based, with an appropriate balance between the instructional program and those activities which provide entertainment and promote better school public relations. In addition, an effective program should provide for continuity (K—12), diversity, and relevance, which will ultimately extend into students' adult lives.

Suggested Class Offerings

Some students will show interest in participating in specialized performance groups and may give evidence of talent in singing or playing an instrument. If music education is to provide these children with opportunities at the elementary level for instruction commensurate with their interests and endowments, they should be offered opportunities for classroom experiences in singing and in the playing of orchestral and social

---

[5]Violet Anselmini Allain, *Futuristics and Education.* Bloomington, Ind.: Phi Delta Kappa Educational Foundation, 1979, p. 11.

[6] *Music in General Education.* Edited by Karl D. Ernst and Charles L. Gary. Reston, Va.: Music Educators National Conference, 1965, p. 205.

instruments. Also, provisions should be made for the more experienced and talented musicians to participate in small ensembles and in advanced choirs, bands, and orchestras. The value of these specialized groups in elementary schools is that they provide children with more than average interests and abilities with appropriate opportunities and challenges. In secondary schools, the performance groups allow young people to develop more refined skills of interpretation, to develop performance skills to a high degree of excellence, and to become acquainted with more advanced music literature.

Instrumental and choral classes are best conducted by music specialists and should grow out of effective general classroom instruction. A properly designed program in performance music will meet a variety of needs and provide an effective means for students to progress from elementary through secondary levels. The curriculum should be sequenced so as to accommodate students' degrees of interest and levels of musical talent, and it should be balanced so as to involve all pupils while providing special programs to meet the needs of the most talented students.

In addition to performance classes, a number of other music classes may be offered. These classes cover the history, literature, and theory of music. They are of value to nonperformers and performers alike and can serve to interest a larger number of students in the music curriculum. Indeed, a well-planned program of general music classes should form the base from which performance classes grow.

A list of suggested music classes is given below. While these classes usually are offered in secondary schools, many are appropriate at all grades in schools where special emphasis is placed on music. Most of the classes can be divided into

beginning, intermediate, and advanced levels as required.

String instruments
Wind and percussion instruments
Mixed instruments
Orchestra
String orchestra
Chamber music
Band
PE/marching band
Wind ensemble
Jazz ensemble
Voice class
Glee
Chorus
Choral ensemble/madrigals
Vocal jazz ensemble
General music
Basic musicianship
Music literature
Analysis of music
Harmony
Theory
Arranging
Composition
Electronic music
Advanced placement music
Independent study
Piano
Organ
Guitar

Student Performance in Public

Student performance in public should take its proper place as a

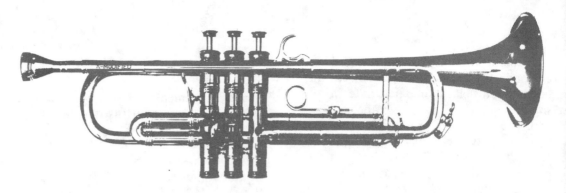

by-product of music education rather than being the purpose for these programs. Student performance should provide an opportunity for a student's successful involvement, personal satisfaction, and joy of participation. This principle relates directly to the selection of music for performing groups. Student performance primarily should provide motivation for careful rehearsing and secondarily should provide positive public relations for the school system. Teachers must avoid performances that exploit student talents.

Providing entertainment is a valid activity of performance groups, but this function should never obscure the basic educational objective—the development of musical understanding.

Schedules for Activities

When preparing schedules for musical activities, one must give consideration to these factors:

- Classroom instructional periods long enough to allow for adequate teaching time in addition to time for distribution and return of materials, tuning of instruments, and removal or rearranging of seats and music stands
- Classes that meet often enough to ensure continuity in learning
- Time of day that does not conflict with a large number of single section classes in other subjects
- In multitrack, year-round schools, arrangement of classes and teacher time to serve all tracks throughout the year as well as to provide for balanced instru-

mentation or voicing in performing groups

Teacher Preparation

The preservice education of a teacher of music should provide for the development of a high degree of musicianship and an understanding of the processes of learning and strategies of instruction appropriate to the ages and abilities of the students to be taught. The curricula of teacher education institutions, therefore, need to be of sufficient flexibility and breadth to provide for the diversity of musical backgrounds, aptitudes, and needs of those preparing to teach music at various levels.

The question of who shall teach music in the elementary school is of prime concern because of the lack of training in music for the majority of classroom teachers. Either in-service and preservice training in music education for the classroom teacher should be increased, or music specialists need to be hired to teach music in the elementary school.

In the past there has been little concern for the qualifications of teachers in the primary grades with respect to music. This is probably because the concepts to be developed at this level are considered relatively uncomplicated. It is important to recognize, however, that the musical experiences of children aged five through eight have the utmost significance in their future musical development. While this situation is true in all areas of learning, it is especially significant in relation to music, for these are the years when children's aural acuity develops most rapidly. Pitch recognition, rhythmic discrimination, musical sensitivity, and attitudes toward music are established in the early years of childhood. Emphasis, therefore, must be placed on developing the musical competence of the teacher who will work with children at the primary level.

One of the greatest needs in music education at the high school level is for teachers who place a high value on music as a part of general education, who are willing to work with students who are less talented than others, and who are dedicated to the proposition that the lives of all young people can and should be enriched by musical experiences that are both emotionally compelling and intellectually challenging. The preparation of such teachers must provide for a thorough knowledge of major masterpieces of music literature, including representative works by contemporary composers. Teacher education programs in music should include preparation for the teaching of music for general education in the courses required for choral and instrumental conductors.

Educating teachers for the areas of specialization that exist in music education requires flexible curriculum at the college level and elective tracks or areas of concentration. In this connection it is suggested that departments of music education maintain a systematic program of guidance counseling which will consistently screen prospective music teachers in order that teachers have an in-depth preparation for the type of position for which they are most suited by ability, personality, background, and interest. This

program should be concerned with both personal and musical qualifications. Performance, interest, and scholarship are, of course, significant factors, as is actual work experience. Significant weaknesses in some candidates' qualifications often do not show up until these students have spent many years preparing for a profession to which they are not really suited. As early as the sophomore year, some form of internship in classrooms at the elementary and secondary school levels might be offered to potential candidates. This experience can make subsequent methods and practice teaching programs much more meaningful than would otherwise be the case.

Music Coordinators

Maintenance of teacher competence and program quality requires constant effort and leadership. For large- and medium-sized districts, the leadership of a qualified music coordinator is essential. Smaller districts, whose needs are just as great, may find it necessary to turn to alternative measures, such as intradistrict support and utilization of a music coordinator. The services of the county music coordinator may be sought by the smallest districts that qualify for direct services.

Music Specialists

According to the Music Educators National Conference (MENC), specialist is defined as "a skilled teacher whose preparation includes substantial work in music leading to those competencies that have been suggested by the MENC Commission on Teacher Education. This would

include the person who has a music education degree as well as one who may have a strong major or minor."[7]

Music specialists can provide the necessary expertise for competent implementation of quality music programs. Such programs recognize:

- The necessity for the establishment of music objectives which meet district goals
- The value of aesthetic education in the lives of individuals
- The significance of the level of instruction provided by specialists
- The value of providing a music specialist for every 600 students enrolled in the district

Staff Development

Music specialists and curriculum coordinators may provide an added dimension to the music program by jointly planning and implementing a regular program of in-service training for classroom teachers. The need for such in-service training has increased considerably over the past decade because of changes in elementary teacher preparation requirements which have minimized the need for college courses in elementary music methods for credentialing. Thus, great numbers of teachers are entering the field without having had at least one methods course in elementary classroom music.

In-service training programs can draw on the expertise of district music specialists as well as guest clinicians from neighboring school districts, colleges, or universities. Professional musicians may also provide expertise and give focus to specific areas within certain in-service training offerings. In addition, community music institutions and agencies may be willing to plan cooperatively with school districts to provide enrichment opportunities for teachers. In all instances when outside expertise is sought, great care must be

taken to integrate these resources with the goals of the staff development program and the music curriculum.

Other resources within the district should be assessed, also. A survey of faculties may reveal teachers with sufficient background and training in music who may be willing to share their expertise through in-service training programs. In addition, these teachers may serve as resource persons for idea exchange programs, teaching strategies, and service on special committees.

Community Resources

Educators should take advantage of the musical resources that can be found in most communities. Adults who are not necessarily professional performers are often sufficiently trained to be able to share their expertise with students. Professionals or former professionals are often willing to volunteer their services. Visiting musicians can enhance and bring into focus concepts already introduced in the regular instructional program. Music educators should, therefore, survey their communities for musicians, both professional and amateur, who would be willing to present musical performances or lectures; encourage their students to take advantage of the musical performances in formal and informal community concerts; bring into the schools local guest artists and clinicians to work and perform with students; and work with their local musicians' union to encourage the use of the Music Performance Trust Fund (where available) to present in-school concerts.

Live Performances

Because of their convenience and easy availability, both the record player and television set have been primary sources of aural and visual experiences for most children. However, neither one can take the place of live performances. Especially in this age of mechanization, children

[7]"The Music Specialist in the Elementary School," *Music Educators Journal*, Vol. 59 (November, 1972), 60.

need to experience the personal contact between the performer and the audience. Live performances of music relate the creator and viewer of the experience on an intimate basis and add an important dimension to the students' responses. Both pre- and postconcert involvement or related experiences magnify live concert benefits.

Promoting the greatest possible interaction between school music education and the most musically significant activities generated by the community is important. No matter how modest community resources may be, the best that is available can be helpful.

Artists-in-Schools Programs

In recent years the practice of having artists perform and teach in schools has increased. Projects funded by the National Endowment for the Arts and the California Arts Council have provided Artists-in-Schools (AIS) opportunities for schools previously unable to provide such programs.

The intent of the AIS program is to "(1) enhance children's powers of perception and their abilities to express themselves and communicate creatively by using tools and skills they would not otherwise develop; and (2) provide an opportunity for artists to function in schools and communities in a manner and under circumstances conducive to their own artistic development."[8]

Plans for AIS may vary from district to district and school to school. However, the most effective programs are ones which provide highly specialized experiences which extend and enrich the regular curriculum. Strong support systems which provide for careful preplanning, practical scheduling, artist-teacher orientation, and a systematic plan for communication, documentation, and

evaluation further guarantee quality programs.

Quality AIS projects may have a very positive impact on school music programs when music educators and professional musicians work cooperatively to broaden the experiences and perspectives of students and teachers.

Students with Special Needs

Music education offers enrichment for the lives of students with special needs, ranging from the gifted to those in special education programs.

Gifted and Talented Students

A report from MENC states that: "Gifted and talented students are capable of a high level of response to musical experiences that are both emotionally compelling and intellectually challenging."[9]

To challenge the intellect and refine the skills of gifted and talented students, music educators must provide musical experiences and opportunities to meet the more

[8]John F. Aguino, *Artists as Teachers.* Bloomington, Ind.: Phi Delta Kappa Educational Foundation, 1978, p. 10.

[9]*Music for the Academically Talented Student in the Secondary School.* Reston, Va.: Music Educators National Conference, 1960, p. 15.

advanced needs of such students. The following opportunities may be provided for students within the context of the regular school program:

- Providing a thorough education in the basic fundamentals of music
- Providing opportunities to perform in a variety of situations
- Encouraging participation in musical ensembles
- Providing opportunities to acquire skills in secondary performance areas
- Giving recognition when others are granted awards for academic and athletic accomplishments
- Providing opportunities to exert musical leadership

As schools further consider programs which extend and enrich the educational opportunities for their gifted and talented students, they may choose from a number of options. Such staffing and programming might include any or all of the following:

- Individualized instruction
- Advanced placement opportunities
- Artists-in-residence
- Teacher assistants
- Nongraded classroom organization
- Specialized groupings
- School/conservatory consortia
- School/symphony orchestra cooperative plans
- School/professional chorale cooperative plans
- School-within-a-school

Programs on an advanced level should provide specific experiences which meet the needs of students who plan to pursue music as a career. The performance level of young musicians today far exceeds the level of a scant 20 years ago. Therefore, students should be encouraged and assisted in performing at their highest level of attainment. Other students who embrace music performance as an avocation, a means for enriching life, and as a leisure-time pursuit should be encouraged as well to continue

advancing in the development of performance skills.

Special Education

The content of music instruction can be essentially the same for children with disabilities as it is for their peers. The rate at which they learn and respond may be different. In many instances, however, handicapped children may participate in the same activities and enjoy the same experiences in regular classroom settings.

Educational opportunities in music for such students should allow for their specialized needs, as teachers nurture and guide these students' musical skills and talents. Trained specialists in music therapy can also provide an added dimension to programs of music for the handicapped.

In some instances current music education books include specific suggestions for activities that are appropriate for mainstreaming situations.

Multicultural Education

Provisions should be made to identify and make accessible to students the variety of music in world cultures to enrich music education. Experiencing the richness and diversity of the world's music deepens a child's perception of various cultures. Every student's heritage is a rich resource

86

for music studies. Musical learning
should not be confined to the limited
acceptance of only the European
model, but should extend to the
cultural heritage of all people.

According to the *Music Educators
Journal,* "The excitement of exploring
other people's ways of life ought to be
opened up to schoolchildren. Then
familiarity can replace strangeness;
respect (and understanding) can
replace fear."[10] The *Music Framework
for California Public Schools* states
that every effort should be made to
research and use authentic examples
of music produced by various cultures.
It is of the utmost importance, however, that all music to be included
in the music education program be
studied first and foremost as expressive
sound; i.e., for its aesthetic value.[11]

Careers in Music

Career education programs in music
must keep pace with the current trend
to infuse career education into the
curriculum at every level. Not only
should these programs become a part
of a child's education on an ongoing
basis, but plans for such programs
should incorporate music career
programs in such a way that they
are a natural component, not a last-
minute afterthought.

Traditionally, music career information has been limited to that which
has had to do with performance or
teaching careers in music. Music
horizons now present unlimited opportunities that need to be explored with
students.

Currently, career education is
initiated much earlier than in the past,
with career awareness programs
beginning at the elementary level. All

too often, however, these new
programs provide very limited
information. Career education
coordinators and music educators
must work together to raise the
awareness level about careers in
music. Not only should students be
made aware of the expanding
opportunities, but parents, school
counselors, principals, and district
level administrators need current,
relevant information about the rich
possibilities of music and music-related
careers. Lloyd Schmidt states, "Career
education in music can bring relevance
to the music lesson. Special classes or
programs may not be necessary, but a
broad concept of awareness is
advocated from kindergarten through
adult education in which the student
can encounter the real world of music
in all of its manifestations."[12]

Career education in music should
not be limited to mere perusal of lists
and job counseling. It should become
interwoven in the curriculum so that
information and experiences provide a
rich knowledge base for the student.
Career education can be a meaningful
component of music education
programs from the elementary level
through the secondary level and
beyond.

---

[10]Christine Crist, Jon Dunn, and Robert Revicki,
"Song as a Measure of Man," *Music Educators
Journal,* Vol. 62 (May, 1976), 35.

[11]*Music Framework for California Public Schools:
Kindergarten Through Grade Twelve.* Sacramento:
California State Department of Education, 1971, pp.
48-49.

[12]Lloyd Schmidt, "The Importance of Career
Education," *Music Educators Journal,* Vol. 63
(March, 1977), 41.

Evaluation of Student Progress

In determining goals and objectives for any instructional program, educators realize that the objectives also are *standards* by which individual student progress can be measured. Therefore, a school's plan for systematic evaluation will call for a clear statement of objectives appropriate for that school.

Because of the subjective nature of music, student progress often appears only in student attitudes and participation during regular class activities. Teacher-made checklists then become the instruments of assessment. Testing of skill development will be based on teacher observation of performances, whether individually or in groups. Acquisition of factual knowledge can be tested by more traditional means. However, all assessments must take into consideration the cultural backgrounds and experiences of the students in order to ensure that the expectations are realistic.

Environment, Materials, and Equipment

An effective music program requires quality materials and equipment as well as a variety of instructional settings. Sufficient up-to-date instructional materials and ample resource materials are critical to the needs of school music programs. In addition, there are certain basic needs that must be met for equipment, space, location, and acoustics.

Selection Guidelines

Guidelines and procedures should be developed by districts to ensure that high quality materials, equipment, instructional media, and facilities are provided. A selection committee can be formed to study and evaluate these items and to make recommendations for purchases. Such a committee should include persons who have an understanding of the needs in the area under consideration (vocal, instrumental, general, elementary, and so forth). In addition, the committee must be given ample time to perform its duties.

The selection committee should consider taking the following steps:

- Study district philosophy and goal statements for music education.
- Consult district courses of study as well as the instructional guides for instruction in music.
- Refer to the state music framework. Use as references the "Music Criteria for Evaluation of Instructional Materials," in the appendix of this document, and current professional music education association literature.
- Conduct a needs survey for the school or district.
- Inventory available material, equipment, instruments, and survey facilities.
- Establish criteria for selecting materials and equipment.

Those who make the final selection of materials, equipment, and facilities should measure the following factors against the criteria that have been established.

Classroom Materials

With rising costs, a realistic appraisal must be made of the kinds of material needed in the classroom. Publishers, for instance, might consider offering alternative or optional plans that provide ungraded books that contain materials appropriate for various experiential, maturational, cultural, and interest levels.

The following recommendations suggest options which may supplement the current practices of schools and districts:

- Adhere to the established cycle for regular purchase of state-adopted textbooks.
- Invest in one copy of all the teachers' manuals and records for all of the music series at each

grade level so that teachers have a wider choice in selecting the material. Provide carts for convenient transportation of the supplies.

- Compile a master file of instructional materials from which teachers may choose. Code the file according to use and relate it to curriculum guidelines.
- Communicate to teachers the availability of resources on district, county, and state levels.
- Offer the necessary staff development for teachers, coordinators, and administrators on the use of state-adopted materials.

Facilities for Music Education

Planners should give special consideration to unique facility requirements of music education, such as:

- Ample, serviceable, and secure storage space
- Appropriate rehearsal space for both vocal and instrumental needs
- Appropriate areas for individual and small group practice

Specific characteristics for both basic and quality programs in music are outlined in publications from the Music Educators National Conference. Examples are *Planning and Equipping Educational Music Facilities;*[13] *Music Buildings, Rooms, and Equipment;*[14] and *The School Music Program: Description and Standards.*[15] These documents provide information which will assist planners in determining such matters as appropriate dimensions, room essentials, types of rooms, desired number of rooms, and acoustical considerations.

[13]Harold Geerdes, *Planning and Equipping Educational Music Facilities.* Reston, Va.: Music Educators National Conference, 1975.

[14] *Music Buildings, Rooms, and Equipment.* Edited by Charles L. Gary. Reston, Va.: Music Educators National Conference, 1966, p. 119.

[15]Paul R. Lebmat and others, *The School Music Program: Description and Standards.* Reston, Va.: Music Educators National Conference, 1974, pp. 33—36.

Equipment for a Program

To achieve the objectives of a music program, one should select good quality equipment. In addition, an adequate budget must be provided for the maintenance, repair, and necessary replacement of equipment.

Standards for selecting equipment are described in the publications that were previously cited from the Music Educators National Conference.

Quality of Classroom Instruments

The quality of classroom instruments is often inferior. The rigorous use that has often been made of these instruments is one reason for lack of concern about them. If the only purpose of an instrument is to give a student something to do, then a noisemaker is all that is needed; however, if instruments are to be used for developing sensitive aural perception and for creating music, the quality of the instrument is of the utmost importance.

Conclusion to Chapter 4

It should be emphasized that this framework recommends music education programs that have substance. Effective programs are organized systematically and sequentially and in a manner that will promote a gradually developing understanding and appreciation of all of the aspects of music and skills with which to perform and create music.

This framework is based on the idea that music education should, indeed, be aesthetic education.

Chapter 5

Visual Arts

Visual arts education is basic to developing fully literate citizens. Educators should work to help students reach a level of visual aesthetic literacy which gives them an understanding of the communicative nature of the visual arts and which provides them with expressive and intellectual skills. The visual arts communicate forcefully and directly. Students who identify and master the symbolic structure of visual arts possess the ability to speak to that part of themselves and others that is not dependent on the coding and decoding of verbal language. This is particularly important in our society, where more information is transmitted visually than verbally.

Students who participate in the visual arts develop a structure for responding to and symbolizing their experiences. These encounters lead to the formation of enduring attitudes, values, and satisfactions. Students will begin to derive pleasure from their accomplishments as they gain flexibility and confidence from having direct experiences with the visual arts.

The visual arts should be included in the school curriculum as learning to see aesthetically, as the creative experience of producing artwork, as a study of the heritage of art, and as the critical study of art forms. Students should have opportunities to experience all four of these content areas within the context of their general education, from kindergarten through high school. There are times when the visual arts, to maintain the integrity of the discipline, should be taught separately; and there are also times when they may reasonably be related to another art form or general subject field. Teachers with limited time and resources will want to find opportunities for interrelating art as well as treating it as a separate discipline with its own body of knowledge and skills.

The visual arts are also a part of basic learning. They provide opportunities for self-discovery and

creative expression for all students. Students in special programs also benefit from experiences in the visual arts. Artistically and/or mentally gifted and talented minors, children with special needs, and those in bilingual-bicultural programs require learning opportunities that enable them to develop and expand their visual and aesthetic potentials.

This framework should help educators in all disciplines fulfill their responsibilities to teach visual as well as verbal skills to all students. It is intended for use by all educators, not just art specialists. As a resource, the framework should assist school staff, advisory committees, and others to develop visual arts curricula, organize teacher preparation programs, evaluate instructional materials for visual arts education, and plan programs to involve students in all of the arts.

Recent educational research strongly supports the teaching of the visual arts in every classroom to every child. As teachers broaden their knowledge of the visual arts and are encouraged by successful experiences with students, they gain competency in working with the discipline.

Teaching the visual arts requires a commitment to students and to an educational program that promotes imaginative thinking and values aesthetic responsiveness.

Selected Visual Arts Terms

In this framework specific terms are used to distinguish parts of the underlying structures of the visual arts. Design is an overarching concept that denotes a comprehensive scheme, plan, conception, or organization: the arrangement of independent parts to form a coordinated whole. This formal organization is achieved through the use and interrelationship of elements and principles. They are referred to as *elements and principles of design* or *art elements and principles of design* or *composition.*

These *design elements,* which are the content of most aesthetic perception activities, include:

Color—Visual sensation dependent on the reflection or absorption of light from a given surface (*hue, value,* and *intensity* being the primary characteristics).

Line—An identifiable path of a point moving in space. It can vary in width, direction, and length.

Value—Light and dark; the gradations of light and dark on the surface of objects.

Shape—A two-dimensional area or plane that may be organic or inorganic, free-form or geometric, open or closed, natural, or of human origin.

Form—A three-dimensional volume with the same qualities as *shape,* or the illusion of three dimensions.

Texture—The surface quality of materials, either actual (tactile) or visual.

Other terms which are not usually classified as design elements but are often used by artists to describe visual qualities further include:

Mass—The actual or implied physical bulk, weight, and density of three-dimensional forms occupying real or suggested spatial depth.

Space—A volume available for occupation by a form; an extent, measurable or infinite, that can be understood as an area or distance, one capable of being used negatively and positively.

Volume—Any three-dimensional quantity that is bound or enclosed, whether solid or void.

Principles of design which are the subject matter for most formal analysis activities include:

• *Balance*—An equilibrium of similar, opposing, or contrasting elements that together create a unity.

- *Symmetry*—A balance in which elements are alike and will appear to demand one another as a line that falls in one direction demands a line that falls in another direction.

- *Asymmetry*—A balance achieved through the use of unequal parts or elements.

- *Contrast*—Use of opposites in close proximity (light and dark, rough and smooth).

- *Dominance*—The difference in importance or emphasis of one aspect in relation to all other aspects of a design.

- *Repetition*—The recurrence of elements at regular intervals.

- *Rhythm*—The regular repetition of particular forms or stresses; also, the suggestion of motion by recurrent forms.

- *Theme and variation*—Some dominant feature repeated with variations to give the work its dominant character.

Unity—The distinguishable units or elements that seem to belong to each other so that each contributes something to the functioning of the whole.

In component one, the term *aesthetic perception* is used to designate a specific aspect of perception. It refers to learning to see the world metaphorically as well as directly; e.g., a tree may be viewed as a symbol which expresses majesty or somberness in contrast to a source of wood for building a structure.

In component three, "Visual Arts Heritage," the term *style* denotes a family of characteristics when applied to a period or school in art. *Style* is an individual mode of expression of an artist.

Components, Goals, and Objectives for Students in Visual Arts Education

The components used throughout this framework relate directly to the goals and objectives of a program in visual arts education.

This organizational base for curriculum development includes:

Component One: Aesthetic Perception—Visual and Tactile

Goal I. To develop and expand aesthetic perception in students so that they may:

- Increase aesthetic awareness of visual and tactile qualities in works of art, nature, events, and objects within the total environment.
- See the world directly and metaphorically by perceiving the physical world in terms of visual and tactile images and symbols which are unique to the visual arts.

Component Two: Creative Expression—Artistic Knowledge and Skills

Goal II. To develop and expand visual arts knowledge and skills to express ideas imaginatively, students must be able to:

- Acquire artistic skills to express and communicate responses to experiences.
- Recognize the importance of personal experiences and respect the originality in their own visual expressions and in the artwork of others.
- Develop manipulative and organizational skills in using visual arts media effectively to translate ideas, feelings, and values.

Component Three: Visual Arts Heritage—Historical and Cultural

Goal III. To acquire knowledge of historical and cultural developments which occur as a result of varying needs and aesthetic points of view, students will be able to:

- Study a variety of artworks and accomplishments of contemporary, historic, and prehistoric cultures.
- Understand that art reflects, records, and shapes history and plays a role in every culture.
- Gain an understanding of their creative abilities and their artistic heritage within the context of a comprehensive world view.
- Clarify their own aesthetic values and learn to appreciate differences in the aesthetic values of others.

Component Four: Aesthetic Valuing—Analysis, Interpretation, and Judgment

Goal IV. To develop a base for making informed aesthetic judgments, students will be able to:

- Make informed responses to works of art, nature, and other objects within the total environment by using objective criteria for analysis, interpretation, and judgment.
- Derive meaning and value from experiences by making and justifying judgments about aesthetic qualities in works of art and other objects within the total environment.
- Use analysis, interpretation, and judgment about visual relationships based on learned aesthetic values to improve art production.

Developmental Level Charts

The following charts are a matrix based on the four components for visual arts education. Vertically, the level columns present a *selected* group of competencies to be achieved by students at a given level. Horizontally, the columns show a group of sequential competencies basic to the selection and organization of instructional content designed for students to achieve specific objectives.

The three levels should be seen as illustrative learning competencies, where Level I is the beginning stage of learning at any age, Level II is the intermediate stage of learning, and Level III is the advanced stage in the visual arts experience.

The examples are intended as guidelines for teachers and district curriculum developers to illustrate some of the steps by which the goals and objectives of visual arts education can be reached.

Component One: Aesthetic Perception—Visual and Tactile

Goal I: To develop and expand aesthetic perception

Objectives: Students will be able to:

- Increase aesthetic awareness of visual and tactile qualities in works of art, nature, events, and objects within the total environment.
- See the world directly and metaphorically by perceiving the physical world in terms of visual and tactile images and symbols which are unique to the visual arts.

Sequential Overview

Students need consistent instructional opportunities to examine a wide variety of forms that are natural and of human origin to develop aesthetic perception. As they interact with these forms, students will reflect upon and talk about their observations and feelings to become more perceptive of the aesthetic qualities. Through these encounters, the range and amount of aesthetic responses are increased and enriched.

Students at level II will participate in a wide range of experiences designed to develop and extend their abilities to identify images and symbols in works of art, natural events, and objects within the total environment that are appreciated in and for themselves.

Level III students will refine their aesthetic perception. They will extend their ways of seeing by learning to select, analyze, and enjoy qualities within works of art, nature, and objects in the total environment that can be characterized as aesthetic. This process of selecting, analyzing, and enjoying is basic to the making of informed aesthetic judgments.

Content/Skills	Level I	Level II	Level III
Recognize design elements.	Recognize and discriminate among the visual characteristics of the design elements (line, color, value, shape, texture, and space) in forms that are natural and of human origin.	Make finer discriminations about patterns of light and shadow, surface treatments, and the interrelationships of these and other design elements when responding to forms that are natural and of human origin.	Demonstrate ability to make refined and subtle discriminations when analyzing the interrelationships of the elements and principles of design.

Component One—Continued

Content/Skills	Level I	Level II	Level III
See underlying structures.	Observe the specific details of design principles (e.g., repetition, rhythm, balance, and variation on a theme) in forms that are natural and of human origin to sense their underlying structures.	Recognize and compare the three-dimensional composition details of forms that are natural and of human origin, as seen from various viewpoints and angles, to become more perceptive of their underlying structures.	Categorize and analyze the three-dimensional qualities of forms that are natural and of human origin to become more aware of the function and purpose of their underlying structures.
Discriminate visual characteristics.	Observe that objects and things look different under varying conditions, such as light, position, motion.	Identify other effects or visual impressions that result from changes, such as unusual positioning of objects and things in space.	Predict effects on visual impressions that result from changes in such conditions as light, distance, atmosphere, position, recurring motion, and new technologies; e.g., lasers and holograms.
Recognize variety in visual and tactile characteristics.	Describe imaginative ways to aesthetically perceive works of art, nature, and objects in the total environment.	Describe imaginative or alternative ways of perceiving the environment to break stereotyped images.	Describe imaginative ways to perceive aesthetically, such as taking multiple or many-faceted views of objects; inventing new labels and positions for objects and things; and speculating on how works of art, nature, and objects in the total environment could look.
Categorize visual and tactile characteristics.	Describe ideas and feelings when observing the visual and tactile qualities in works of art, nature, events, and objects within the total environment.	Describe visual and tactile qualities and how they are organized in works of art, nature, and objects within the total environment.	Identify and describe visual and tactile qualities that exist in significant works of art and analyze how they are organized to communicate expressive content.

Content/Skills	Level I	Level II	Level III
Respond aesthetically to visual and tactile characteristics.	Discuss impressions of works of art, nature, events, and objects within the total environment using descriptors that identify observed visual and tactile characteristics.	Use descriptors, similes, and metaphors to describe unique visual and tactile characteristics observed in works of art, nature, and objects within the total environment.	Use descriptors, analogies, and metaphors to describe unique interrelationships observed in works of art, nature, and objects in the total environment.
Analyze aesthetic perceptions.		Compare differences between general perceptions used in everyday living and aesthetic perception.	Analyze the unique characteristics of aesthetic perception as compared to those of general perception as they reflect upon the quality of everyday life.

Component Two: Creative Expression—Artistic Knowledge and Skills

Goal II: To develop and expand visual arts knowledge and skills to express ideas imaginatively

Objectives: Students will be able to:

- Acquire artistic skills to express and communicate responses to experiences.
- Recognize the importance of personal experiences and respect the originality in their own visual expressions and in the artwork of others.
- Develop manipulative and organizational skills in using visual arts media effectively to translate ideas, feelings, and values.

Sequential Overview

Throughout Level I, students engage in drawing, painting, designing, sculpting, constructing, printmaking, and crafts. These activities involve the process of selecting, arranging, and decision making. Students will need a wide variety of experiences with art media. Information on the careers in the visual arts should be introduced.

Students at Level II will continue to work with such visual arts processes as drawing and painting, constructing, printmaking, crafts, graphics, film animation, and environmental design. They will increase their skills in working with art media to express ideas, feelings, and values. Originality should be an essential requirement. Students will also continue to develop knowledge related to careers in the visual arts.

Visual arts experience for Level III students includes opportunities to broaden special art interests and to continue the process of transforming personal experiences into art forms. They should refine their skills in working with art media and learn to value their own efforts to think imaginatively. Some will consider the possibility of art careers as a professional field of work.

Content/Skills	Level I	Level II	Level III
Use artistic skills.	Demonstrate ability to use drawing and painting techniques to organize and depict ideas, feelings, and moods.	Demonstrate ability to use drawing and painting techniques (shading, brush drawing, dry and wet brush, or mixed media) to organize and depict ideas, feelings, and moods.	Demonstrate a control of drawing and painting techniques that adds craftsmanship to the personal statement.

Content/Skills	Level I	Level II	Level III
Apply design elements and principles.	Demonstrate ability to design by using overlapping shapes, variation in lines, colors, sizes, and textures to work with such design principles as balance, dominance, and repetition.	Demonstrate ability to design objects and things used in everyday living, such as fabrics, wrapping paper, tools, furniture, and mechanical devices using design elements and such principles as repetition, balance, and variations on a theme.	Demonstrate ability to design using elements and principles of design to solve environmental, industrial, and commercial problems in creative ways.
Express three-dimensional qualities.	Demonstrate ability to model, to construct by joining forms, and to carve by taking away material.	Demonstrate ability to model shapes into representational and abstract objects; to construct by joining a variety of forms to make objects and simple sculptures; and to carve by using hand tools to directly cut away materials using three-dimensional media.	Demonstrate ability to model by using add-on and sculptural techniques, such as scoring and combining forms; to construct through the use of techniques, such as soldering, bending, molding, and welding; and to carve, using hand and machine tools.
Create in print media.	Make a print using either built-up or carved surfaces to make impressions on another surface.	Make a relief or intaglio print by using such design elements as combinations of shapes, colors, lines, and textures and such design principles as balance, dominance, and unity.	Produce a print using woodcut, etching, lithography, or serigraph process to develop a concept using various techniques involving variation in thickness or thinness of line.
Create in craft media.	Demonstrate ability to work with such craft processes as weaving, modeling, and stitchery to make objects that demonstrate beginning levels of craftsmanship.	Demonstrate ability to apply design elements and principles, using skills in craftsmanship in such craft processes as weaving, constructing, stitchery, batik, or jewelry.	Produce a craft object, using the knowledge of elements and principles of design, the characteristics of the medium, the requirements for functional use, and the technical skills involved in good craftsmanship.

Component Two—Continued

Content/Skills	Level I	Level II	Level III
Create in the graphic arts.	Produce graphic symbols, signs, and posters using design elements and such principles as balance and contrast to communicate ideas and feelings.	Produce graphic symbols, signs, posters, or wall designs to communicate an idea, sell a product, or create a decorative effect.	Produce a graphic design, using lettering and illustration to communicate to a specific audience; plan and execute two-dimensional wall designs to create optical illusion or spatial impact.
Create in the photographic medium.	Illustrate with a camera such concepts as selective subject matter and the effect of light and motion on visual images.	Produce still photographs, film, television, or animation sequences, utilizing design elements and such design principles as rhythm, variation on a theme, and balance to communicate ideas of realism, illusion of movement, or story content.	Demonstrate the ability to utilize design elements and principles with still photography, filmmaking, television, or animation sequences to communicate ideas of reality, fantasy, history, or contemporary problems and issues.
Utilize environmental design.	Demonstrate ability to arrange objects in space.	Produce an environmental design, using elements and principles of design to illustrate new ways to organize space.	Demonstrate the ability to use design elements and principles to plan an imaginative environment accommodating different life-styles.
Recognize career opportunities.	Understand that careers in the visual arts exist and that artists use knowledge to create works of art and objects used in everyday living.	Identify and investigate the range of visual arts careers and the knowledge, skills, and attitudes required to work effectively.	Evaluate educational opportunities in the visual arts and prepare a portfolio of original artwork.

Component Three: Visual Arts Heritage—Historical and Cultural

Goal III: To acquire knowledge of historical and cultural developments which occur as a result of varying needs and aesthetic points of view

Objectives: Students will be able to:

- Study a variety of artworks and accomplishments of contemporary, historic, and prehistoric cultures.
- Understand that art reflects, records, and shapes history and plays a role in every culture.
- Gain an understanding of their creative abilities and their artistic heritage within the context of a comprehensive world view.
- Clarify their own aesthetic values and learn to appreciate differences in the aesthetic values of others.

Sequential Overview

Students at Level I should learn about art heritage in terms of contemporary times and places. Learning about artists, their contributions, and ways of communicating cultural values and beliefs of people through the visual arts will be essential areas for study.

Students at Level II will add to their general knowledge of art heritage by learning that each culture has its own aesthetic values. The creative art efforts of a culture (the paintings, architecture, ritual artifacts, and objects used for daily living) are influenced by the culture's aesthetic values as well as by social, political, and economic factors. An important learning outcome from this study should be a deeper appreciation of their own aesthetic values and those of other people and cultures.

A study of art heritage should give Level III students deeper insights into the role that the visual arts have played in the development of cultures throughout the world. Learning to clarify their own aesthetic values and appreciate differences in the values of others is a fundamental part of this study. The roles and contributions that artists and other people with specialized arts interests have made and the development of style by individual artists are representative of content areas to be studied.

Content/Skills	Level I	Level II	Level III
Recognize varying cultural themes.	Identify themes in selected works of art from various cultures.	Identify some of the symbols that different cultures use to portray common themes.	Compare a theme in works of art from different cultures.

Component Three—Continued

Content/Skills	Level I	Level II	Level III
Analyze the creative process.	Describe a variety of visual art forms produced, using the vocabulary of visual arts media.	Recognize that artists, such as painters, sculptors, architects, designers, filmmakers, and craftspeople often make art by conceiving an idea, elaborating and refining it, and finally giving form to the idea with art media.	Recognize differences between ways that artists talk or write about the creative process and their work and ways that historians, curators, critics, and anthropologists describe particular works.
Recognize the artist's role.	Recognize work produced by individual artists.	Recognize the role of artists in the community.	Identify the role of artists who have achieved regional, national, and international recognition and ways that their works have influenced thinking.
Recognize varying cultural styles.	Identify artworks of the same style from a group of artworks.	Recognize that works of art have a general cultural style that reflects the people's values, beliefs, particular ways of perceiving the world, and levels of technology.	Identify the general style and period of major works of art and relate social, political, and economic factors that influenced the works.
Discriminate national cultural styles.	Recognize style in selected contemporary American works of art.	Identify works of art selected from various American ethnic backgrounds which illustrate variation in style.	Discuss contemporary style trends in American art as reflections of diverse developments in our culture.
Recognize the function of visual arts in a community.	Describe ways that people are involved in the visual arts within a community.	Identify uses of the visual arts in business and industry, including architectural and commercial design, advertising, television, film, and the art careers associated with all of these forms.	Identify the variety of art forms used in business and industry and the vocational and professional fields used to communicate these forms.

Content/Skills	Level I	Level II	Level III
Recognize visual arts from world cultures.	Recognize selected works of art from a variety of world cultures.	Distinguish among art from major cultural areas of the world, including Europe, Africa, Latin America, and Asia, and from different periods in time.	Analyze differences in media used by various cultures and relate these findings to visual arts achievements.

Component Four: Aesthetic Valuing—Analysis, Interpretation, and Judgment

Goal IV: To develop a base for making informed aesthetic judgments

Objectives: Students will be able to:

- Make informed responses to works of art, nature, and other objects within the total environment by using objective criteria for analysis, interpretation, and judgment.
- Derive meaning and value from experiences by making and justifying judgments about aesthetic qualities in works of art and other objects within the total environment.
- Use analysis, interpretation, and judgment about visual relationships based on learned aesthetic values to improve art production.

Sequential Overview

Aesthetic perception involves learning to see in the manner of the artist, through direct interactions with the environment, popular and serious works of art and objects used for daily living. Students at Level I develop aesthetic perceptions by learning to use such thinking skills as observation, discrimination, comparison, contrast, and imagination. Classroom instruction in these early aesthetic interactions provides a base for making informed judgments.

Developing the ability to make aesthetic responses requires consistent interactions with works of art, nature, and objects in the total environment. Students need opportunities to build their capabilities in learning to analyze, compare, and search for relationships as a means of continually learning to make more informed judgments. Learning to talk about works of art requires opportunities and encouragement to use language in expressive ways at Level II.

Level III students will develop a degree of expertise in learning to make informed aesthetic responses. They should work in greater detail with questions of meaning as they interact with their own art and works of art by professional artists. Students' interests in individual artists and their art forms should be encouraged and shared so that insights into aesthetic responses are broadened and enhanced.

Content/Skills	Level I	Level II	Level III
Analyze design elements.	Use design elements (line, color, value, shape, and texture) to describe works of art, nature, and other objects within the total environment.	Make distinctions in design elements when describing works of art, nature, and objects in the total environment.	Identify the relationships among design elements that give the work of art a particular emphasis and/or sense of unity.

104

Content/Skills	Level I	Level II	Level III
Recognize use of design elements.	Identify some ways in which design elements may be organized, using design principles that include repetition, rhythm, balance, and variation on a theme.	Select artworks that are similar or different in the way design principles are organized.	Describe how design principles contribute to the expressive qualities of a work of art.
Recognize art media and processes.	Identify specific media (oil, watercolor, clay, wood, stone, metal) that are used to create works of art and other art forms.	Discuss a process related to a medium, such as watercolor, clay, or weaving, and how it is used in producing a work of art.	Explain ways that artists, as individuals, use selected art media. Explain how artists who represent a particular style use selected art media.
Recognize artistic mood.	Describe the portrayal of ideas, feelings, and mood in a work of art.	Describe the meaning of works of art in terms of mood, sense of tension, conflict, and relaxation expressed through the formal organization of the design elements, and the expression of selected ideals, such as courage, power, and wisdom.	Discuss the meaning of a work of art and make judgments about the aesthetic qualities that can be supported by identifying relationships among the design elements and principles.
Describe aesthetic characteristics.	Talk about design elements in artworks, nature, and objects in the total environment using descriptors, such as adjectives and adverbs.	Use descriptors, similes, and metaphors to describe visual characteristics observed in works of art, nature, and objects in the total environment.	Use descriptors, metaphors, and analogies to describe visual characteristics of works of art, nature, objects in the total environment, and those that may be temporary, such as earth works.

Content/Skills	Level I	Level II	Level III
Discriminate artistic style.	Look at two artworks of similar style or media and recognize that the two works are not identical.	Compare two artworks of similar style or media to identify qualities that make these works similar or different.	Compare two or more artworks of similar style or of the same artist and identify those qualities which make those similarities apparent.
Analyze aesthetic similarities and differences.	Look at two artworks of the same subject; e.g., portrait of a child, by different artists, and be able to recognize differences in the organization of the art elements.	Compare two artworks with the same subject matter but different in media, artists, and styles, and describe the qualities that make those artworks similar or different.	Compare two or more artworks of different media, artists, and styles, and analyze those qualities which make those artworks different or similar.
Recognize artistic characteristics.	Be able to differentiate between an art reproduction and an original work of art.	Use an art reproduction to identify the medium from which an original artwork was made and talk about visual cues used to make decisions.	Describe in aesthetic terms what makes one work of art greater in quality than another.
Recognize aesthetic characteristics.	Use visual arts terms to describe the aesthetic and unaesthetic elements in a specific urban or rural environment.	Compare two environments and describe the qualities that make them aesthetically similar, different, pleasant, and/or unpleasant.	Compare two environments and analyze in aesthetic terms the qualities that make one environment more appealing than the other.

Program Development

Those developing a visual arts program need to consider certain essential aspects of such a program: curriculum planning, program results, student exhibitions, time and scheduling, teacher preparation, staff development, human resources, and community resources.

Curriculum Planning

This framework provides a basis for individuals and districts to develop specific art curriculum objectives. Objectives may be accomplished by making a sequence from (1) general goals for education; (2) general goals for visual arts education; (3) objectives for grade levels and/or courses; (4) objectives for units within courses; to (5) behavioral or learner objectives for activities within units. Next, student activities should be devised to enable students to reach the objectives, and then the means for assessing growth should be developed.

Each of the components should be considered when objectives are being written. Every lesson need not incorporate them all; however, none should be neglected. Objectives, as specified in this document, can be selected according to the level at which students are able to work. Units may be developed which utilize general themes and which incorporate specific objectives from each of the component areas. Each of these objectives must then be broken down into a set of behavioral or learner objectives around which student activities may be planned.

A sample theme might be "The Environment." From "Component One, Aesthetic Perception—Visual and Tactile," competency number one at Level I might be chosen:

To recognize and discriminate among the visual characteristics of the design elements (line, color, value, shape, texture, and space) in forms that are natural and of human origin.

To explore the environment, students could be guided on a walk through their neighborhood. A possible behavioral or learner objective for this competency would be the following:

Given a photograph, sketch, or list of round and square objects in their neighborhood, students will be able to compare them to similar shapes in specific works of art.

When learner objectives have been completed, appropriate student activities need to be planned. Each activity may utilize one learner objective or incorporate several. Learner objectives will overlap, but emphasis will change as new themes are explored.

Program Results

The visual arts offer knowledge and understandings about visual aesthetics that can be acquired through no other studies. An aesthetically literate citizen is the desired "end-product" of a strong visual arts education program. Learning can be recognized at ascending levels as students progress through well-planned programs that incorporate the components, goals, objectives, knowledge, and skills of visual arts. At each level students should experience an extension of their *intrinsic satisfaction*—their internalized learnings and feelings about the visual arts.

As a result of experiences which develop *aesthetic perception* through the visual and tactile modes, students will:

- Find pleasure in making subtle discriminations of visual characteristics and qualities.
- Derive pleasure in analyzing and describing visual phenomena.
- Enjoy the changing aspects of visual phenomena.
- Be flexible in selecting a point of view.
- Delight in metaphorical thinking.
- Pursue growth in the vocabulary related to visual art.

- Be aware that aesthetic perception is a highly individualized cultivation of the senses *and* the intellect.

Through *creative expression* with art media and techniques, students will:

- Develop insights about the importance of visual art in their lives.
- Achieve the sense of freedom to create which comes from technical competence.
- Seek the pleasure there is in being surrounded by well-designed and aesthetically pleasant environments.
- Exhibit confidence when responding to requirements for good artistic technique.
- Enjoy subtle differences in print techniques.
- Enjoy the personal freedom and selectivity available in the use of photography in daily life.
- Be aware of the effect of space use on the quality of life.
- Find satisfaction in the process which produces effective communication through graphic design and video media.

- Evidence an appreciative attitude toward the work of others.

Through exposure to the *historical and cultural* expressions in the visual arts, students will:

- Appreciate variations in style as an expression of the individuality of artists.
- Learn to value cultural similarities and differences in the expressions of others.
- Seek to know and understand artists in the community as they interpret the various themes of their cultures.
- Achieve pleasure from a visit to an art museum or cultural event.
- Develop an abiding respect for the diversity of cultures as seen in their visual art.
- Develop an openness to the artistic expressions of contemporary American artists.
- Develop a genuine respect for the contributions of all professional artists in the community.

Through ongoing experiences requiring *aesthetic judgments,* students will:

- Exhibit spontaneous responses to design elements as aesthetic sensitivity becomes intuitive.
- Seek life-long involvement in visual arts experiences.
- Find pleasure in the accurate articulation of design elements seen in visual arts products.
- Exhibit an awareness of artists' styles that becomes a source of personal enjoyment.
- Interpret the meaning in visual arts products in a highly personalized manner.
- Find pleasure in making choices about visual arts products based on well-founded, personal aesthetic judgments.

Intrinsic satisfactions for students at all levels naturally result from effective programs in the visual arts. The possible satisfactions listed above are often not observable and usually cannot be evaluated. They represent, however, the enduring value of visual arts education.

Student Exhibitions

Student art exhibitions and displays are a natural outcome of creative work in the classroom. They provide opportunities for students to see their own work and that of others and to use these experiences to analyze and evaluate their own visual statements. Displaying original artwork is a source of personal satisfaction for students, because it is a means of recognizing quality in ideas, in visual presentation, and in artistic technique. In addition, this process involves parents and other community members in a part of the educational process which gives insights into the purposes and outcomes of visual arts programs.

An exhibition schedule needs to be planned so that exhibits and displays are a consistent part of the educational program. Sites, such as galleries in schools, libraries, and community centers, need to be utilized for student exhibitions. Other related activities should include training students in methods of preparing an exhibition and developing a student docent corps.

Time and Scheduling

Effective visual arts instruction calls for regular, planned, and sequential learning opportunities and for lessons with expanding content and utilization of diverse teaching strategies.

Flexibility of scheduling is essential in providing for variations in individuals, in time blocks, class size, and instructional content. For example, the requirements for time and space for the following activities will differ: a 20-minute discussion of a recent exhibition, a 90-minute studio work session, a brief review by a small group of an art concept or process, a humanities presentation to a large group utilizing multimedia techniques, and a demonstration by a visiting artist. Scheduling should provide for independent short-term units as well as for courses conducted on the basis of a week, a quarter, a semester, or a year. School administrators need to develop new approaches to scheduling. And individual differences must always be considered when new programs are being developed.

To provide adequately for visual arts instruction, district and site administrators should:

1. Work with staff to bring about a more effective utilization of time and space to achieve the objectives set for the elementary visual arts program and the students being served.

2. Consider alternative ways to schedule visual arts programs, such as modular scheduling, flexible scheduling, individualized instruction, independent study, instruction by units, contractual programs, and other efforts to maximize the use of time.

3. Require one year of art for all junior high school students and

offer differentiated scheduling patterns that are suited to various types of art programs and various groups of students.

4. Establish a graduation requirement of one year of studio art or art history for every high school student.

5. Provide staff development programs in the visual arts to help teachers develop strategies to make the most effective use of time, space, equipment, and materials.

Teacher Preparation

The decision as to who shall teach visual arts, and with what educational training, determines the quality of art experiences provided for children in the school. The success of any program to educate children and youth depends on competent teachers who are supported by adequate resources of professional quality.

Visual art education of general elementary teachers has been, for the most part, inadequate. Since college and university art courses are not required as part of the elementary credential program, teachers have tended to depend largely on contacts with art supervisors, or other art resources, and the sharing of information with members of their own teaching staffs.

At the high school level, the majority of art teachers are graduates of a professional art education program in the visual arts. In addition to this education in the visual arts, most of these teachers have had training in understanding the adolescent.

All teachers need to continue acquiring understandings of the psychology of children and adolescents as well as of the behaviors involved in learning to create visual art, to respond to the environment, to perceive, to symbolize, to abstract, and to design. A thorough knowledge of and affection for children will lead

to teacher-student relationships that make learning vital and relevant. Teachers must have the ability to communicate effectively with students of diverse ethnic backgrounds and, especially, with students from impoverished families and those whose mother tongue is a language other than English.

Competence in teaching art requires skill in art expression, art criticism, and knowledge of art history and culture.

Institutions of higher education need not only to offer instruction in the total content of art education but also to provide teachers with strategies of teaching for the effective use of an increasing range of resources that enhance learning. Teachers also need to have adequate knowledge of research and assessment in art education.

Staff Development

The continuing education of teachers requires the consideration of a number of aspects:

- Teachers, consultants, and administrators, as professionals in a field that is constantly undergoing change, must develop new ways to refine and achieve goals in developing art programs. At all grade levels such persons serve as guides, leading students to develop powers of creative and critical thinking. Attitudes and skills are developed which enable students to understand their cultural heritage and provide them with bases for making aesthetic judgments.

- Teachers must continually redefine their goals and increase their capacities for achieving their objectives. They should become effective in the areas of (1) leadership; (2) communication; (3) decision making; (4) problem solving; (5) creativity; and (6) cooperation. All of these processes apply to the teaching of art.

- By continuing their education, teachers keep up with the intellectual, social, and technological trends of the times. To keep teachers prepared, they need special assistance from many sources—from within the school district, from the business and cultural areas of the community, from institutions of higher education, from offices of county superintendents of schools, from learning laboratories throughout the state, and from national associations or agencies.

In-service education has proven beneficial to teachers for a number of reasons:

- Analysis of in-service education programs indicates that teachers change in direct proportion to their personal involvement. The coordinated efforts of teachers, consultants, and other specialists needed to make curriculum improvements are dependent upon quality resources and time allocations, both of which are essential to a continuing educational program.
- Methods of meeting the need for continuing education of teachers will vary. One possibility is released time for teachers (which is especially productive when it occurs at times when teachers are not physically, emotionally, and intellectually tired from a full day with students). Other times are staff meetings designed to deal with particular issues, workshops, demonstrations, and visits with colleagues. Courses at local colleges or through extension divisions continue to be a principal source of in-service growth. Cultural experiences, such as seminars with museum personnel, or planned meetings with recognized artists and study at an art center should be encouraged. Teachers will also benefit from professional reading

and participation in the National Art Education Association (NAEA) and the California Art Education Association (CAEA) through their workshops, conferences, newsletters, journals, and research publications.

Human Resources

The addition of teachers with special training in the visual arts to elementary school staffs is a beneficial trend for education. Art specialists can be utilized effectively not only to strengthen visual arts instruction but also to bring an increment of flexibility and broader modes of learning to other curriculum areas.

The responsibility for maintaining quality programs in the visual arts at both the elementary and secondary levels falls to the individual teacher, with strong help and support from school district and site administrators.

Building Administrator

For effective leadership, the administrator should:

- Develop a better understanding of visual arts programs by attending arts workshops and arts advisory committee meetings, making frequent class visitations and inquiries about art programs, and having arts demonstrations by arts staff members for the faculty.

- Support visual arts programs through the best possible scheduling of arts teams' meetings and of student arts classes and programs.
- Support visual arts programs through adequate staffing.
- Support visual arts programs by providing sufficient equipment and supplies and adequate physical facilities.
- Support visual arts programs through budget allocations, which are consistent throughout the district, for materials and equipment.
- Support visual arts programs on a financial basis that is equitable in terms of the support given other disciplines.

Supervisor and/or Director of Curriculum and Instructional Services

The role of this person in a school district is one of ensuring a district-wide visual arts program. The supervisor should:

- Provide continual support and commitment for the visual arts.
- Clarify responsibilities of the coordinator, staff, principals, and district in their relationship to the visual arts program.
- Be informed about the structure of the visual arts as a discipline.
- Provide continual leadership in the organizing of staff development programs in the visual arts.
- Work toward a balanced curriculum which includes the visual arts.

Visual Arts Coordinator

In addition to providing curriculum development and leadership of the visual arts staff, the coordinator should have a continuing role in the selection of personnel, allocation of budget, evaluation of teachers, and implementation of the program. The

coordinator must also work with community arts' resources as well as with other decision makers on the school district's administrative staff.

Community Resources

In addition to the regular classroom program of visual arts, art programs should provide a variety of resources and activities for general enrichment. These might include the following:

- A gallery collection of changing professional art exhibitions
- Lectures and demonstration programs by adults from the visual arts community; e.g., a critic, museum curator, collector
- Specialized study trips to museums, galleries, artists' and designers' studios, showrooms, manufacturing centers, and other appropriate art-related businesses and institutions
- Referral of students to appropriate out-of-school art classes, workshops, seminars, and clubs
- Opportunities for student work experiences in professional art fields

- Opportunities to observe public art and local architecture
- Opportunities for special programs in the visual arts during summer vacation and in the after-school hours
- Opportunities for cooperative experiences with local colleges and universities
- Participation in artists-in-the-schools programs

Students with Special Needs

Visual arts education offers enrichment for the lives of students with special needs, ranging from the gifted and talented to those in special education programs.

Gifted and Talented Students

The brightest and most talented individuals have the task of deciphering the past, developing the present, and designing the future. Legislation passed in 1980 allows school districts to allocate gifted and talented programs state monies for arts education for gifted students. It (1) allows for the identification of,

and enhanced learning opportunities for, artistically talented students; and (2) permits the inclusion of arts education components in the school programs of academically gifted students.

Artistically gifted students who show high-level ability in the expressive, critical, or historical aspects of the visual arts must be encouraged to pursue the development of these potentials. For some students, appropriate, intensive work in the visual arts should be arranged through special scheduling. Some examples of other enrichment activities are special classes, college and university classes, art museum programs, contact with artists, opportunities to instruct younger children, and exploratory work experiences with designers and craftspeople employed within the business community.

Many academically gifted students are also artistically talented, with the potential to become able artists and performers, designers, historians, or critics. Some are not. The personal discipline required to be an effective learner in the visual arts is very demanding. Some gifted students, whose intellectual curiosity is enormous, will make the personal commitment to self-disciplined learning that is required to achieve satisfactions providing incentives for continued progress. Gifted student program leaders need increased awareness of reachable goals as a prime requisite for continued motivation and learning in the discipline of art. Learning readiness and student interest, ability, and potential should all be determinants in the selection of gifted students who will participate in special visual arts instruction.

Programs for these students should provide in-depth studies in the roles and contributions of the artist, art critic, historian, curator, archaeologist, collector, restorer, exhibitor, architect, and environmental designer. The goal of these studies is to focus on the historical and contemporary

contributions of visual artists to discover the significance of their work.

Special Education Students

The visual arts are an avenue for providing successful experiences for children with special needs. They offer alternative forms of learning to see, to know, and to respond to experience. The four visual arts components and objectives should serve as a basis for developing special programs. These children, like all children, need a sequential program of instruction that provides activities which focus on worthwhile learnings.

Strategies for implementing programs will depend on the nature of children's limitations. Some children will have visual arts instruction as part of their mainstreaming experience. In making this transition, the classroom teacher and the special education teacher will need to have frequent conversations to arrive at the least restrictive environments for these children.

In other situations children will need a visual arts instructional program which has undergone specific modifications. These modifications will require a careful analysis of art processes for the purpose of identifying various conditions that

need to be changed so that children can work successfully. For example, certain modifications may need to be made in helping a student to use a specific tool (or material), work space may need to be expanded, or specific steps in an art process may need to be broken down into smaller units with shorter periods of work time. There may be situations in which children will need to experience the visual arts as therapy so that their confidence can be restored and they will be encouraged to do something with art media, tools, and materials. In cases where a special use of the visual arts is contemplated, children should work with qualified art therapists.

Another strategy involves the sharing of art resource services. In these situations, where the art resource teacher is responsible for the program, other teachers will need to work with the special education teacher to plan appropriate instructional content and ways of working with children.

Multicultural Education

Studying works of art from various world cultural groups provides students with an understanding of the important role that the visual arts play in communicating the values, beliefs, rituals, mores, desires, and hopes of a particular group of people. Students will also discover that visual art forms are often the only enduring historical and cultural records that present the progress of ideas and feelings of people.

Purposes for multicultural studies in the visual arts include:

1. To teach, through direct contact with authentic images and artifacts, the essential aesthetic qualities that are characteristic of objects and structures of a given culture.

2. To highlight, through the use of varied resources, the uniqueness of the cultural heritage while

demonstrating its similarities to our own culture.

3. To enlighten children about people's needs, which are basically the same, even though different cultures express their beliefs, values, goals, rituals, and customs in unique art forms.

4. To demonstrate that a basic drive in human beings is to create artistically. This is evidenced in the art products from the earliest to the most recent technologically oriented civilizations.

5. To show that the visual arts of all cultures are worthy of study, appreciation, and value. The visual arts of cultures from which this society emerged are relevant to our current life, because they are links to our origins, guideposts to our future, and starting points for new ideas. Today's advanced communication and transportation technologies place people in such close proximity that the future of humanity depends on mutual understanding and respect.

Multicultural studies involving the visual arts may be taught as an area of historical/cultural study or as a part of social studies and/or language arts programs. Some guidelines to follow in organizing instructional content in these areas include:

1. Sufficient ethnic artifacts which exemplify the symbols, motifs, workmanship, and materials of the culture being studied should be available.

2. The art forms should be studied within the historical/cultural context in which they were produced.

3. Aesthetic qualities, such as types of materials, workmanship, colors, textures, patterns, and imagery, need to be pointed out so that children learn to "read" the art forms and motifs

indigenous to the culture to determine, with confidence, the characteristics of never-before-seen artifacts of a culture.

4. A specialized vocabulary needs to be developed so that the aesthetic qualities of a culture can be stated accurately.

5. A broad variety of secondary resources, such as films, slides, photographs, and books on a variety of cultures, must be available so that students are exposed to the authentic images of representative cultures.

6. The teacher needs to deal with the symbolic meanings of the artifacts or art forms presented, so that children can be helped to search for accurate information and learn authentic concepts and generalizations about specific cultures.

Careers in the Visual Arts

In our society many visual arts careers exist because of the high value placed on the impact of the visual image. Designers of such things as clothes, advertising, automobiles, interior decoration, toys, furniture, business machines, television, and graphics reflect our primary concern with visual images when new products are developed. A matter of economic reality is that efficiency and utility often take a secondary role to visual impact in the designing of articles for commercial production.

Several hundred visual arts and art-related careers and occupations are listed in the *Dictionary of Occupational Titles*. These listings suggest that the visual arts cut across a broad spectrum of occupations in our society. Some visual arts careers allow artists to work as independent contractors in their specialized fields. Professional painters, sculptors, architects, landscape designers, aerial photographic interpreters, restorers, film editors, silversmiths, model makers, biological photographers, medical illustrators, and many others may be included in this category. A broad group of visual arts professions also involves curators, critics, arts managers, researchers, and translators of primary art documents who study, interpret, or respond to the visual arts.

New careers in the visual arts are emerging and expanding with technological innovations and the constantly changing needs of people. Such professionals as urban planners and structural engineers, astrophysicists, computer program designers, and plant physiologists draw heavily on visual arts knowledge and skills.

Students need to be informed about the contributions the visual arts make to economic stability. This can be accomplished through art career education curricula, which also inform students about possible careers in the visual arts. Such courses should develop an awareness of how aptitudes for art relate to earning a livelihood in the world of work. Students also need to recognize how reading, writing, speaking, and computing skills affect the attainment of visual arts career goals. They need to learn how to work on an art task with and without supervision. A belief in the values of commitment to one's task, punctuality in meeting deadlines, sustained effort, and careful craftsmanship should also be developed.

Art career education at the primary level should acquaint students with a variety of people whose work involves knowledge in the visual arts, including book illustrators and designers of clothing, furniture, toys, everyday utensils, and packaging for all kinds of consumer goods. Even young children can investigate how their work in paint and clay might be related to the activities of book illustrators and makers of dinnerware.

Students at the intermediate levels should learn how people's interests and knowledge influence their career decisions. They can begin to

categorize occupations into clusters, such as industrial, commercial, professional, social service, and the arts. They can gather information about a particular career and find examples of an artist's portrayal of any subcategory of this career. They might produce an art product with this career as their theme. They should also learn that an interest in art developed through school activities may carry over into leisure-time activities or become an avocation.

High school students can investigate the value of artistic endeavors for both individuals and society. They should also explore many media and ideas to discover and develop their own visual arts talents and interests. Students also must develop relevant analytical and critical skills by studying artworks and through interaction with adults engaged in careers in the visual arts. By the conclusion of their high school education, students can make tentative decisions about specific areas for their development in art and nonart-related careers.

Evaluating Student Progress

Evaluation in the visual arts should be a constant and ongoing process. Evaluation should be individualized, emphasizing both the subjective and the objective aspects of the learning process. Consideration should be made regarding the growth and development of a student's skills, understandings, attitudes, and abilities to respond and express himself or herself both verbally and visually.

The ways of assessing a student's progress might include a variety of methods and techniques, such as:

- Expressive measures—Students' responses demonstrate visually a command of material, organizational skills, and expressive abilities.

- Observation of students—Teachers make objective and subjective judgments, based on their observation of student behavior, including attitudes, interests, enthusiasm, originality, and independence.

- Performance tests—The results of students' performance tests reveal their values, their ability to perform a certain task, or their attitudes. Students' performance in producing an artistic, personal expression reflects their ability to organize and express ideas and feelings.

- Individual inventories—Students' responses on an individual inventory reveal their preferences or attitudes toward certain learning activities.

- Perception tests—Students' responses to visual and tactile materials verify their abilities to perceive.

- Skill tests—The results of skill tests make possible an assessment of students' ability to use specified skills, including both technical and physical skills, and their ability to make aesthetic decisions that are based on these skills.

- Objective tests—Students' responses to oral or written questions demonstrate their knowledge.

- Subjective tests—Essay assignments encourage students to demonstrate their ability to think through problems, applying their total experience to their solution rather than merely repeating what they have been told.

- Verbal tests—These tests allow students to express orally or in written form their substantiated opinions, knowledge, and judgments.

- Self-evaluation—This process involves students in the assessment of their own progress and deserves special attention. Students need help in learning to

assess accurately their own growth.

- Checklists—These lists are used to identify students' preferences for certain types of activity, their estimates of the effectiveness of the instructional program, their selection of vocabulary, their likes and dislikes in their total art experience, and their suggestions for improving the instructional experience.

Environment, Materials, and Equipment

Visual arts experiences can foster a comprehension of life that goes beyond everyday awarenesses. Students also can learn to make creative and sophisticated visual expressions. When students create, they observe, explore, respond, decide, select, interpret, define, and know; the environment for this activity must be stimulating, appealing, and supportive. The general conditions necessary for successful visual arts programs of high quality are the following:

1. A psychological atmosphere conducive to experimentation:

   - The teacher must recognize and respond to the characteristics of individual students in realistic ways.
   - There must be opportunities for students to work at their own pace, interpret their perceptions in several ways, and, if they regress, to recover and redo.
   - There must be opportunities for students to work independently with ample time to explore, discover, and express the inherent possibilities each art material presents as they learn to make a statement concerning themselves in their world.

2. A physical environment arranged for learning:

   - Classrooms should be of adequate size, with appropriate

lighting and sufficient space for frequent changes of educationally stimulating visuals. Examples from the environment, as well as the work of artists and children which relates to current lessons, should be displayed.
- Sufficient work space and clean-up facilities must be provided for both planned and spontaneous art activities.
- Students need to have access to a wide variety of quality materials for three-dimensional work, such as fabric, yarn, wood scraps, cardboard, clay, and metal. Similarly, they need a broad variety of quality supplies for their two-dimensional art: paints, crayons, pastels, pencils, and appropriate tools. Supplies must be attractively sorted and marked so that children can work independently when necessary.

- Materials and equipment must be in good condition to allow children to achieve their maximum expression safe from hazardous situations.
- Children need a storage area which is secure from vandalism so that they can build a collection and record of their artistic progress.

Instructional Media

In an age when much of our information comes through widely varied media (photographs, movies, video images, and prints), these aids should be a part of visual arts programs.[1] Students and teachers need access to quality audiovisual equipment and supplies in sufficient quantities so that these may be used appropriately for both instruction and as art media. School districts should provide adequate equipment for preparation and viewing and should purchase instructional materials, including:

- Art reproductions
- Educational television films
- Filmstrips
- Slides
- Videotapes
- Videodiscs

Conclusion to Chapter 5

This visual arts framework provides the continuity and sequence for building effective visual arts programs. Neglecting any aspect at any level can result in failure to achieve the goal of producing aesthetically literate citizens. Reviewing existing art programs is the first step. Then procedures for curriculum development and instructional change should begin, following the guidelines described in the preceding pages.

---

[1]The state has adopted "Criteria for the Selection of Instructional Materials in Visual Arts" for kindergarten through grade eight. This section, included in the appendix, should be consulted by those who select printed and nonprinted instructional media.

Chapter 6

Interdisciplinary Education Involving the Arts

This section includes suggestions for interrelating the arts and for integrating one or more of the arts with other areas of the general curriculum. The illustrations are meant to be merely examples of the content and procedures that might be used.

Relationships Among the Arts

According to Daniel C. Jordan, "Working with relationships across disciplines rather than within them always produces new perspectives and insights."[1]

A viewpoint toward the arts is critical in making curriculum decisions. It is important to recognize that there is no body of knowledge identified as "interdisciplinary relationships in the arts."

Each of the arts has its own unique content and system for making aesthetic responses. The identification of similarities among ideas, skills, cultural aspects, and/or values provides the opportunity for developing teaching strategies. As curriculum planners work with the idea of interdisciplinary relationships among the arts, each arts discipline should be recognized also for the uniqueness of its content. Commonalities should not be forced; although the word is the same, the concept of "shape" as it is used in the visual arts has technically different meanings in music, dance, and drama. Through effective teaching, students can learn to recognize both the similarities and the differences; and in the process, their understanding of each content area will be extended and deepened.

To teach by using interdisciplinary relationships, one must discover and utilize some of the basic connections between and among the arts. These

[1]Daniel C. Jordan, "The Arts—Neglected Resources in Education," in *Controversies in Education.* Edited by Dwight W. Allen and Jeffrey C. Hecht. Philadelphia: W. B. Saunders, 1974, p. 39.

connections are identified through statements that describe some of the unique characteristics of the arts as distinct from all other subject matter disciplines and through concepts common to all the arts disciplines.

Statements that describe the distinct characteristics of the arts include:

- The arts provide unique ways of knowing oneself and the world.

- Learning the language and structure of the arts enables the individual to deepen levels of participation as an artist, performer, and/or responder.

- Images, sounds, movement, and words are unique ways of presenting the ideas, feelings, hopes, desires, aspirations, and fantasies that are manifested through the arts.

- The arts expand possibilities for imaginative thinking by developing and drawing on an individual's mental bank of images, sounds, and movement.

In working with any one of these statements, the curriculum planner will need to examine those sections in each of the framework's chapters that contain discussions of these specific aspects of each discipline. It is from this systematic study of each discipline that the interdisciplinary relationships become apparent.

The quest then should be for the identification of those interdisciplinary concepts which make it possible to draw legitimate connections between the arts. For example, when dealing with elements, such as color or texture, the overarching interdisciplinary concept is that an art form can be analyzed, understood, or appreciated in terms of its *organization.* It is this kind of abstract concept, *organization,* that should be the focus of the instruction rather than attempts to show that these elements have some common meaning in each art form.

Each of the arts disciplines involves both impressive and expressive experiences. The impressive mode has to do with encounters with any one of the arts that require visual, tactile, and/or auditory skills. Listening to a concert, viewing a piece of sculpture, a dance, or a theatrical production are examples of the impressive (input) mode.

The expressive mode involves creating, making, and/or reproducing an art form. Writing a play, choreographing a dance, painting a portrait, and composing or playing a piece of music are examples of expressive (output) experiences.

A group of common concepts is clustered around each of these modes. As a suggested way of organizing for those who work with these concepts in each of the disciplines, the following questions provide guidelines to appropriate content for study:

Concepts: creation, invention, production

Where do composers, artists, playwrights, and choreographers find ideas to use in creating a work?

What steps do these creators follow in producing a work?

How do creators decide that a work of art is complete?

Concepts: performance, recreation, interpretation

How do performers select the work they perform?

What do performers use as a guide for recreating a work?

What do performers do when they interpret a work of art?

How do performers decide on the quality of their performance?

Concepts: historical/cultural style, significance

What are the clues in the work that enable an arts historian to analyze a work?

What were the social, political, economic, and personal conditions that influenced the work?

How is this work related to other works that make it an example of a style or period?

Is the work a bench mark?

Concepts: appreciation, value

What vocabulary is used to describe works of art?

What is the central idea, theme, or mood of the work?

How has the creator organized the work to express ideas and feelings?

What new understandings, appreciations, or insights are brought to the work?

According to Elliot Eisner, "The development of literacy in the use of one symbol system bears on the development and use of literacy in other symbol systems. Cognitive processes interact, and incompetence in any one of those symbol systems exacts a price that exceeds the borders of its own cognitive domain."[2]

Interrelated Arts Experiences

Designing Interdisciplinary Studies Programs states that: "An interdisciplinary approach to learning combines or interrelates aspects of at least two academic disciplines or subject areas," utilizing the content, the principles, or the procedures of the disciplines.[3] A concept or topic being developed in one art area may be reinforced by introducing related material in one or more of the other arts. Teaching about the element of rhythm in music, for example, can be strengthened by searching for

differences through comparison and contrast; e.g., repeated patterns in visual art and repetitive movement in dance and drama/theatre. Then the integrity of each discipline is maintained and enhanced. Such an integrative approach makes for more efficient and effective learning. The "vignettes" which follow illustrate some ways of organizing instruction so that each of the arts expands and extends learning in the arts. These sketches are exemplary of ways to interrelate the arts.

Vignette, Level I. Consider the effectiveness of a multidisciplinary way of teaching a principle, such as "repetition," which is important in several arts disciplines. In music a call and response song involves repeated patterns of sound. In drama/theatre or dance, accompanying each syllable of a person's name with a specific motion can be responded to with a similar set of motions; and, finally, both may be repeated to form larger patterns. In art a potato print pattern repeats a design created with shape and color.

Guided listening experiences based on a selection such as Paul Dukas' *The Sorcerer's Apprentice* may generate several activities that reinforce the principle of repetition. The theme that is repeated throughout the selection may serve as a basis for student choreography and/or improvised movements which illustrate repetition through motion. This represents an interdisciplinary approach organized around a common concept which is expressed through unique organization of elements and principles in each of the arts. All of these experiences can build and reinforce the idea of repetition by focusing on the unique features in each discipline.

Vignette, Level II. An example for organization around a topic is offered by the following Level II vignette, using the poem *Jabberwocky* by Lewis Carroll. The teaching approach could,

---

[2]Elliot Eisner, "Why Public Schools Should Teach the Arts," *New York Education Quarterly*, Vol. 11 (spring, 1980), 2—7.

[3]*Designing Interdisciplinary Studies Programs: A Project Search Development.* Albany: University of the State of New York, Division of Humanities and Arts Education, 1976, pp. 5—7.

of course, be modified to suit the classroom situation.

Visual Arts: "What do these characters look like? Big, small, fat, skinny? What color and texture are they? How are they dressed? Could you paint a picture of them or create a costume for each one?

"What environment would they live in? Is it sunny or dark and scary or cold and muddy? How could we change our space to build such an environment?"

Music: "What sounds would we need? Could we make them with our voices and bodies? Are there harsh sounds, soft, ringing, or clicking sounds? Do we want recorded music? What kind of rhythm should it have? Do we need a melody? What kinds of instruments might we use? How could the music enhance the excitement of the story?"

Dance: "How will the characters move? Let's experiment and exaggerate the movements to show whether they are large or small, smooth or angular, according to the personality of the character. Will your character's movement be fast or slow, sustained, vibrating, or swinging?"

Drama: "Let's look again at the story and find the most important parts. Are there conflicts? Do we need to follow the poem word for word? Should each person speak separately or as a chorus? How does each one feel? How could we communicate those feelings through pacing and tone? Should we rehearse or improvise? Let's try both ways and then talk about what we have created."

Vignette, Level III. At Level II, students can plan cooperatively to do a topic-centered activity, perform it, and then evaluate what they have experienced. Level III students are capable of a greater sophistication in selection, planning, executing, and evaluation. The experiences might originate in a common concept, such as the style of Expressionism, or a literary topic involving a variety of intellectual and expressive learnings, such as the true story *The Diary of Anne Frank.*

Planning by teachers of arts disciplines within a school can produce rewarding results. After some lessons on Expressionism, class members in dance, music, and the visual arts can plan to work simultaneously on a project to discover how to represent the style of Expressionism in the arts. While students in the orchestra, band, chamber orchestra, or other musical ensemble play music in the Expressionistic style (e.g., Stravinsky, Schoenberg, and so forth), art students paint with tempera colors on large panels in response to the music, employing the appropriate aspects of style and composition. As the painters create Expressionistic designs in line and color, the dancers improvise movement inspired by the sounds and visual designs. They must observe the elements of dance by effectively using space, time, force, and shape in improvisations, responding to the characteristics perceived in the music and emerging art work. Drama/theatre is added by the dancers' speaking words at random, with the emotional quality of Expressionism, improvising verbally as they move.

Another approach at Level III is described as follows:

The play *The Diary of Anne Frank* deals with the theme of man's inhumanity to man. Advanced drama/theatre students may select and prepare a short scene from the play for presentation to other students.

Dealing with the same theme, other students may study the powerful visual statement made by Picasso in *Guernica* and share their observations and learnings with the total group.

Still others may wish to work with a listening selection, such as Verdi's *Otello* or Stravinsky's *L'Histoire d'un Soldat,* and narrating the story that led to the music or perform a part based on the story.

Using the film *The Green Table,* a fourth group may choose to study the choreography that is used to express the theme in this antiwar ballet by Kurt Joos.

In this manner these students can gain insights into how the different arts give form to a common idea.

The Arts and Other Disciplines: Integrating the Curriculum

The connections made between the learner's store of sensory experiences are vital to the comprehension and interpretation of information. The arts not only provide the sensory experiences and the images and symbols upon which the learner will rely, but they also contribute significantly to students' conceptual and skill development.

Recent trends have shown an increased effort by educators to define the "basics" in broad terms so that the term *basics* embraces ways of learning rather than specific subject areas to be learned. This rationale is based on the accepted fact that knowledge is developed in many ways. Concepts are formed by a variety of sensory and cognitive modalities. Experiences encountered through the diversity of the numerous disciplines create interests that begin to build relationships between abstract concepts and that which is real and relevant to students. The incorporation of other disciplines into a particular area of study enhances and broadens that study experience. Some of these programs are called "humanities" or "integrated studies." Consider a few examples:

Reading/Language Arts. Concepts, such as space, direction, quantity, sequence, dimension, and likenesses and differences are necessary to the development of reading/language skills. In instances when these concepts are not developed, student learning is seriously impeded. For instance, prereading skills require the sensory experiences which will ultimately become the connectors for forming necessary visual relationships.

Science. The arts offer numerous possibilities for providing appropriate supplements to the development of certain concepts in the study of science. Consider the connections between the arts as they relate to the following desired learner behaviors in science:

- In science the learner "differentiates constants from variables and identifies correlational changes."[4]

- In music, the same learner identifies an ostinato as it is performed in accompaniment to an improvisation.

- In dance, movement represents unity and variety, constancy and change.

- "Units of matter interact. Interdependence and interaction with environment are universal relationships."[5]

---

[4]*Science Framework for California Public Schools: K—12.* Sacramento: California State Department of Education, 1978. p. 31.

[5]Ibid., p. 85.

- In the visual arts, the learner compares artwork using only naturally occurring media with artwork using synthetic media. The artists develop new materials to use in producing artwork.

- In music the learner collects, compares, and categorizes environmental material for use as a producer of musical sounds.

Social Studies. As an embodiment of society's forces, the arts can provide a natural avenue for learning about our kaleidoscopic heritage of history and beauty.

The following examples illustrate various experiences in the arts which can complement social studies programs:

- In music the learner studies the relationship between the African "talking" drums and the language patterns of the people, determines whether this custom has emerged in any other part of the world, and examines the drum as a communicator in other cultures.

- In the visual arts the learner examines the unity and diversity evidenced in maskmaking in world cultures, determines the variety of uses to each of the cultures, and traces and compares the separate histories of maskmaking.

- In drama the learner examines and compares the rituals of life and death as they are dramatized by various cultures and looks for implications in contemporary rituals.

- In dance the learner examines the historical significance of dance in a variety of cultures, compares male-female roles (in dance) from culture to culture, and discovers strands of similarities to be found among the dances of world cultures.

According to Abraham H. Maslow, "Esthetic perceiving and creating

and esthetic peak experiences are experiences seen to be a central aspect of human life and of psychology and education rather than a peripheral one."[6]

Mathematics. The interrelationships between the arts as they deal directly with mathematical studies do not require artificial or unnatural assimilation into the curriculum. For example:

- In music the learner studies musical sounds by examining the mathematical ratios of high and low tones produced in varying lengths of tubing.

- In art the learner examines the intricate mathematical designs in nature, such as the logarithmic spiral seen in the spiraled flower, a nautilus's shell, elephants' tusks, and even canaries' claws.

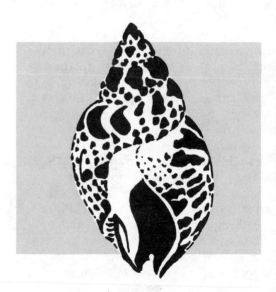

In answering the ancient question of why and how people learn, psychologists and other scientists have concluded that, with adequate and appropriate stimulation and motivation, one's ability to learn is limitless. Learning, they have found, is not confined to certain inflexible, set situations but occurs under a variety of stimuli, in diverse situations, and

[6]Abraham H. Maslow and others. *Perceiving, Behaving, Becoming.* Washington, D.C.: National Education Association, 1962, p. 141.

by differing means of communication with the senses. The interrelationships between the arts and other disciplines exist and need only be examined carefully for effective inclusion.

Rene Descartes demonstrated his awareness of the interrelationships of various branches of knowledge when he wrote: "... all things to the knowledge of which people are competent are mutually connected in some way."

Using the Arts to Teach Content in Other Disciplines

Learning is an integrative process. In a balanced curriculum, opportunities for students to use what is learned in one discipline to clarify or enhance an idea, concept, or skill in another occur almost daily. As learners work across the disciplines, there are many opportunities to discover relationships that lead to the process of forming ideas and concepts. This way of learning provides an intellectual stimulation involving thinking, feeling, and doing behaviors that enable students to be more flexible and inventive in their approaches to problem-solving processes.

A key factor in this approach to learning is the need for students to acquire enough prior experience and knowledge in one discipline to make applications in another. For example, teaching a language arts unit on newspaper communication may require techniques for the visual organization of information on graphs, diagrams, and charts. Ways to present these forms may be suggested by visual arts experiences. Working back and forth between the disciplines reinforces concepts and skills in each of the disciplines. A visual arts class working on advertising layout may benefit greatly from language arts instruction on techniques for writing a compressed message. Both of these experiences require prior learning so

that students feel satisfaction in the quality of product they are able to create.

One of the most pervasive ways the arts can affect learning in other disciplines is by creating a generally positive learning environment.

Students perceive school as a more desirable and exciting place when the arts are an integral part of learning. When the arts appeal to their interest and imagination, students are stimulated intellectually and emotionally. To maximize learning, teachers will need to plan ways to integrate the arts into the curriculum so that they are a basic part of the instructional program. The following are ways of using the arts to motivate, enhance, and enlighten learning and other disciplines:

Idea, Concept, and Skill Development

An art form may be used to introduce an area of study or a concept; for example, using role play or simulation to dramatize an historical event or an economic concept, such as supply and demand. An art form may also be used for idea or concept clarification, such as using a problem in the visual arts involving scale to clarify the mathematical principle of ratio.

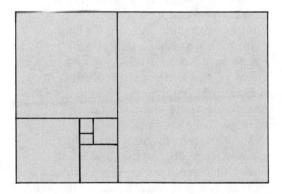

Golden Section

Skills develop more readily as a student applies techniques acquired in one area toward learning content of another, such as clapping a rhythmic pattern to match a mathematical sequence.

Cultural and Historical Connections

Ideas or concepts may be introduced from one discipline to set another discipline into its authentic cultural/historical context. For example, a social studies focus on the effect of the industrial revolution in the United States may be enhanced by examining the content or themes in paintings of that period.

Visual art forms may be used to analyze symbols, myths, and metaphors that are used in a particular culture to communicate the values and beliefs of the people. The lyrics of an American Indian song may be used, for example, to analyze the meanings associated with the sun, corn, and so forth.

However, consider carefully two ways of correlating music and social studies in a study of the American Indian. First, suppose songs of the American Indian are taught by rote and sung by the students at some appropriate time. Although there may be some value for improved understanding of the Indian culture in this practice, there is very little gain in the understanding of music or the similarities and differences between music of the American Indian and music of the Western European culture. The second way would involve much more study of the unique qualities of Indian music—the style and vocal characteristics, kinds of instruments, lack of traditional harmony, intricacies and meaning of rhythmic patterns. Correlation activities depend heavily on the way in which they are conceived, organized, and presented by teachers. Ideally, such instruction will be based on meeting objectives in *both* curriculum areas.

Enduring Values Studies

A multidisciplinary approach involving all the arts may be used to study a broad societal value, such as democracy, courage, justice, beauty, interdependence, or family. In the study of a value, each of the arts develops concepts that lead to the formation of broad generalizations that are inherent in the value.

Designing Interdisciplinary Arts Experiences for Enduring Values

Abraham H. Maslow states that, the best way of teaching, "whether the subject is mathematics, history, or philosophy, is to make the students aware of the beauties involved."[7]

In planning interdisciplinary arts curricula, it is valuable to design

[7]Abraham H. Maslow, *The Farther Reaches of Human Nature.* New York: The Viking Press, p. 31.

learning experiences that relate not only to each component of arts education—perception, expression, heritage, and aesthetic values—but also to the continuum of developmental levels. Always, the desired outcomes of aesthetic education should be the intrinsic satisfactions that outlast the immediate moment and become part of one's system of values. The ideas presented in the illustrations that follow are intended to suggest these kinds of experiences.

Working in an interdisciplinary style provides many opportunities and benefits, not the least of which are:

- The continual discovery of new ways to focus on the integration of content and strategies of teaching
- The facilitation of learning, building on the interests and abilities of students

- A more imaginative, stimulating, and rewarding approach to teaching and learning

The charts that follow indicate some ways that a teacher might integrate the arts with, for example, a multicultural unit in social studies. Activities are grouped according to the levels of sophistication of the students and attend to the components, aesthetic perception, creative expression, cultural heritage, and aesthetic values. Possible outcomes are listed as intrinsic satisfactions, or enduring values. Similar activities could be developed, of course, to relate the arts to other areas of the curriculum.

Social Studies: Multiculture and Dance—A Study of Gesture

Components	I	II	III	Enduring Values
Aesthetic perception	Observe and explore everyday gestures of hands, legs, and whole body.	Discuss and improvise ways that everyday gestures convey meaning.	Discuss and analyze various stylized forms of gesture, as in pantomime, ballet, jazz dance, and so forth.	Awareness of the many facets of gesture
Creative expression	Explore various kinds of gestures freely in structured improvisations.	Create short dance studies that convey emotional states through abstracted movement and gestures.	Choreograph a dance based on a dramatic theme, with the idea clearly communicated through abstracted and stylized gestures.	Enjoyment of creative dances with abstracted gestures
Cultural heritage	Observe and explore the ways that different cultures use gestures.	Discuss and explore the effect of clothing on cultural movement and gestures.	Compare and contrast stylized gestures in other cultures, such as Kabuki theatre, Balinese puppet theatre, European folk dance forms, or Peking opera.	Understanding of the cultural differences in gestural language as nonverbal communication
Aesthetic values	Observe the line of gestures in motion.	Discuss the aesthetic qualities inherent in common and stylized gestures.	View and discuss the use of gestures in a dance and evaluate them according to the aesthetic principles of form.	Appreciation for the beauty and expressiveness of human gestures

Oral Language and Drama—Rhythmic and Vocal Patterns

Components	I	II	III	Enduring Values
Aesthetic perception	Demonstrate a rhythmic pattern by clapping. Listen to recordings of famous speakers and poets and discuss their dramatic qualities, such as pitch, tone, and rhythmic patterns.	Discuss voice interpretation and improvisation, using intonation, postures, and emotions to communicate feelings.	Discuss various playwrights and how they use dialogue to create characters, mood, settings, and so forth.	Understanding the diversity of language and how it is used in a drama/theatre context
Creative expression	Create or practice both rhythmic and vocal patterns. Read simple poems and explore levels of speech, tone, and rhythms (sticky, choppy, punchy, melodic).	Improvise a scene based on an incident from real life, a story, a poem, an object.	Rehearse and share with the class various scripted scenes that use different styles of dialogue; then critique them.	Awareness of the styles in drama/theatre and how each style attempts to communicate ideas, mood, and setting
Cultural heritage	Listen to the vocal and rhythmic patterns that exist in all languages, cultures, and music, and talk about them.	Develop, discuss, and act out your own characters and situations, based on topics in history, literature, or multicultural studies.	Analyze how the *who, what, where, why,* and *when* of any drama production that crosses culture, time, and peoples touches, the feelings universal to us all.	Appreciation for the many contributions that different cultures have made towards developing dramatic literature
Aesthetic values	Make choices based on listening to various rhythmic and vocal patterns, in terms of dramatic quality, tone, and feeling.	View and critique each other's improvisations in terms of aesthetics (feelings, settings, mood, characters).	Analyze and critique the drama/theatre productions of experienced performers.	A working knowledge and enjoyment of dramatic literature (poetry, plays, improvisation, creative drama)

Social Studies: Multiculture and Music—The Pentatonic Scale

Components	I	II	III	Enduring Values
Aesthetic perception	Perceive the musical quality of a Chinese five-tone scale.	Understand the component steps that comprise a pentatonic scale.	Become aware of the use of the pentatonic scale as it is performed with a variety of Chinese instruments.	Enjoyment of music based on the five-tone scale
Creative expression	Play a simple two- or three-tone accompaniment to selected Chinese folk songs.	Perform pentatonic scale patterns and simple melodies.	Perform pentatonic pieces from various Chinese eras.	Appreciation for the variety of Chinese melodies based on the pentatonic scale
Cultural heritage	Become aware of the existence of pentatonic scales in a variety of cultures.	Compare the differences between Asian and Occidental melodies based on the pentatonic scale.	Examine the factors which contribute to the differences in selected examples of Asian and Occidental music.	Understanding of the differences evident between Asian and Occidental music
Aesthetic values	Develop an appreciation for melodies based on the pentatonic scale.	Become aware of stylistic elements inherent in Asian melodies.	Recognize pentatonic elements inherent in American folk music.	Valuing both Asian and Occidental melodies as sources of listening and performing pleasure

Social Studies: Multiculture and the Visual Arts—Oriental Brush Painting

Components	I	II	III	Enduring Values
Aesthetic perception	Perceive line quality through exploratory brush painting with water on chalkboard.	Perceive and discuss line in nature, particularly in trees and branches.	Perceive line in diverse examples of urban environment; e.g., wires, steel structures emphasizing line.	Awareness and enjoyment of line as a habit
Creative expression	Make brush line designs in pairs on large paper, sensing relationships of line.	Make line drawings of trees and branches with brush.	Make line drawings of a city environment, with emphasis on wires and linear structures.	Awareness of variations in line quality in environment
Cultural heritage	Look at simple Oriental line paintings and "trace" lines in the air.	Examine Chinese landscape paintings with a sense of their serene universality.	Examine contemporary paintings by Tobey, Pollock, and so forth, as well as Oriental artists, for their unique use of line.	Understanding of the varied use of line by artists
Aesthetic values	Sit quietly and let eyes follow the lines of an Oriental painting.	Discuss aesthetic elements in Chinese painting as they illustrate aesthetic principles.	Discuss individually the aesthetic use of line in the works of Pollock and Tobey and Oriental painters.	Enjoyment of line qualities of artwork and the environment as an intrinsic value

Parallel Objectives for the Arts and Other Disciplines

The arts integrated into the general curriculum give impetus to learning. When they naturally and reasonably supplement and interact with another subject for mutual benefit, they may effectively be taught together.

The pages that follow provide some *examples* of how objectives for reading/language arts, social studies, science, and mathematics parallel, in many cases, objectives for the arts. By teaching the lesson that meets the arts objective, a teacher may support the related objective in the other subject area. All objectives have been selected from the appropriate frameworks. For each subject area, parallel objectives have been drawn from only one of the arts; in many cases, similar examples could be drawn from any of the other three. Additional lesson activities may be designed to supplement and extend these samples and thus could become the structure for a teachers' guide to interdisciplinary arts education.

Science Objectives:

Show curiosity about objects and events.
- Take an active role in solving social problems related to science and technology.
- Value the scientific contributions of human beings from various historical and cultural groups.
- Show a willingness to support data and ideas against the criticism of peers.

	Objectives	Strategies
Dance		
Aesthetic perception	Verbalize and execute movement vocabulary based on the elements of dance fundamentals (integrating body with spatial, temporal, and energy concepts).	Explore a given area of space by touching, seeing, hearing, and sensing. "Transfer" that given area of space and reproduce its characteristics in a new space.
Creative expression	Use the creative process of dance through exploration, improvisation, problem solving, and inventive thinking.	Create a group dance based on the mechanical workings, design, and sound of a computer.
Cultural heritage	Recognize the universality of dance as language in the past, present, and future.	Through movement depict a discovery of scientific significance from a selected country, such as Mexico, Egypt, or Greece.
Aesthetic values	Develop skills of constructive criticism and make judgments about the aesthetic quality of works of dance as dance relates to communication and to expression of self, others, and life.	Illustrate through movement, working in small groups, the basic principles of electromagnetism. Discuss the validity of the scientific facts presented. Compare and contrast the interpretive elements of the abstracted movement.
Drama/Theatre		
Music		
Visual Arts		

Reading/Language Arts Objective:

- Respond to many kinds of literature on a personal level; become aware of purpose and techniques.

	Objectives	Strategies
Dance		
Drama/Theatre		
Aesthetic perception	Develop an understanding of movement as the external expression of an internal idea, intention, or feeling.	Talk about how body expression reflects feelings.
Creative expression	Experience playmaking which is structured and planned, played, evaluated, and replayed.	Use the playmaking process to create playlets of fables, myths, ballads, fairy tales, tall tales, and biographies.
Cultural heritage	Develop an ability to respect and appreciate various cultures.	Relate the type of literature to a specific culture.
Aesthetic values	Evaluate informal playmaking.	Critique positively each other's contributions.
Music		
Visual Arts		

Mathematics Objectives:

- Develop an understanding about the use of diagrams or drawings to organize and analyze information.[1]
- Use tables or graphs to organize and find new information.[2]
- Examine examples of graphs and diagrams devised during earlier periods in history and from a variety of cultures.
- Exhibit a willingness to present and support collected data to peers.

	Objectives	Strategies
Dance		
Drama/Theatre		
Music		
Aesthetic perception	Demonstrate understandings which will lead to the effective use of written notation.	Investigate the way in which contemporary composers have used drawings and diagrams for scoring compositions.
Creative expression	Communicate musical ideas effectively through the use of notation.	Score a composition with standard notation and another with drawings and diagrams.
Cultural heritage	Understand the purposes and functions of historical (and cultural) situations which have influenced the composition, performance, and selection of music.	Examine ancient examples of notating music and compare with contemporary scales.
Aesthetic values	Use aesthetic criteria for determining the organization of an original composition.	Conduct a performance of an original composition, using a selected scoring system for critical analysis by student peers.
Visual Arts		

[1] *Mathematics Framework for California Public Schools*, Sacramento: California State Department of Education, p. 41.
[2] Ibid.

Social Studies Objective:

- List likenesses and differences among selected cultures to demonstrate that human beings have more similarities than differences. The focus is on exploring cultural differences and similarities as they might relate to art objects produced by Asian, Mexican, and black Americans. Folk art objects are used for study because they reflect some of the cultural values of these groups and because they provide a source of authentic material.

Objectives	Strategies
Dance	
Drama/Theatre	
Music	
Visual Arts	
Aesthetic perception	
Describe unique visual and tactile characteristics observed in works of art and nature and objects within the total environment, using descriptive similes and metaphors.	Use a collection of folk art objects or photographs of art objects from two or more cultures to learn to use art objects as a source of cultural information. Identify and describe the characteristics of each piece; e.g., unique shapes, colors, lines, textures, use of pattern. Talk about and make a list of some of the likenesses and differences in cultural values reflected in these objects; e.g., symbols of power, love of family, relationship with nature, and observance of rituals, celebrations, and religious beliefs.
Creative expression	
Demonstrate the ability to model spheres, coils, and slabs into representational and abstract objects; to construct by joining a variety of forms to make objects and simple sculpture; and to carve by using hand tools to directly cut away materials using three-dimensional media.	Make a simple bowl shape, using clay, and experiment with different ways that decorative patterns are used in each of these cultures to express values; e.g., birds, flowers, sun, power of a god.

Objectives	Strategies
Cultural heritage	
Recognize that works of art have a general cultural style that reflects the people's values, beliefs, levels of technology, and particular ways of perceiving the world.	Examine folk art objects and/or photographs to learn about the style that characterizes each of these cultures. Study objects from one culture, such as Mexican masks, pottery, and basketry to make inferences about the cultural values of these people.
Aesthetic values	
Compare two art works of the same subject matter but different in media, artists, and/or styles, and describe the qualities that make those art works similar or different.	Compare the folk art of two cultures, such as Mexican and Japanese, that may be made from different media like clay and paper, and make a list of similarities and differences. Read to learn how the natural resources of a country and the values of the people have contributed to the uniqueness of the cultural art objects from each group.

Support and Strategies for the Interdisciplinary Approach

According to Rudolph Arnheim, "Twentieth century teachers believe that art is not a privilege of a few people, but a natural activity of every human being; a genuine culture depends less on the rare geniuses than on the *creative life of the average citizen* (italics added); and that art is an indispensible tool in dealing with the task of being."[8]

Planning the Interdisciplinary Curriculum in Today's Schools

Students now in our schools need a curriculum that will prepare them for life in the twenty-first century when computer terminals will make the vast store of human information accessible everywhere. They will require much more than the verbal-analytical skills that dominate in today's schools. The attitudes, appreciations, and modes of thinking cultivated by the arts may be the prime necessities of life 20 years from now. A balanced curriculum, infusing the arts in every aspect of the school curriculum, would stimulate students to a higher level of learning today and would produce a citizen better prepared for adult life tomorrow. Teachers need to consider the potential contribution of the arts to each subject as they make their daily instructional plans.

Enthusiasm is a basic ingredient needed to energize a program integrating the arts at any school level. Conviction that children will achieve at a higher level academically and have fewer absences when the arts are emphasized is confirmed by examples, such as the arts magnet schools in Oakland, California, and the schools in Mesa, Arizona. *Try a*

New Face[9] gives additional details on these and other programs for making the arts integral to the curriculum.

Administrative flexibility and support are also needed if planning is to extend beyond a single, self-contained classroom. For example, in the Grace M. Davis High School in Modesto, California, a program integrated with the arts was planned to meet the junior year American literature and history requirement. Two-hour blocks of time in the schedule and teachers willing to trade classes with each other made this program possible.

Time for planning is another basic necessity. Team teaching requires professionally secure, knowledgeable individuals who can plan enthusiastically and flexibly with their colleagues to interrelate the arts or infuse them into other subjects.

The value of interrelating the arts with all aspects of the school curriculum can be supported by research. Brief examples are given as follows:

In a Wayne State University preschool experiment, children acting out fairy tales (thematic fantasy) or real-life experiences scored about ten points higher than a control group of children who had merely listened to fantasies. In a four-year follow-up study, children who participated in this program showed superiority in a concept learning task in the third and fourth grades. They were also superior in controlling impulsive behavior.[10]

Integration of intellectual learning with artistic participation is advocated by Earl J. Ogletree in "A Curriculum for Two Modes of Consciousness." He feels that children should be encouraged through movement to

Beautiful

美
術

Skill

The Chinese word for ART

---

[8]Rudolph Arnheim, *Toward a Psychology of Art.* Berkeley: University of California Press, 1966, p. 337.

[9]*Try a New Face: A Report on HEW-Supported Arts Projects in American Schools.* Washington, D.C.: U.S. Department of Health, Education, and Welfare, 1979.

[10]"Imaginative Play Enhances Later Learning Behavior," *Brain Mind Bulletin,* Vol. 4 (November 20, 1978), 1.

experience a straight line, curved line, circle, and open and closed figures. This experience can form the basis for later writing letters and numbers, artwork, and, ultimately, (abstract) geometry.[11]

Sheila Ostrander and Lynn Schroeder found that rhythmic musical accompaniment to reading a foreign language to be learned by students, followed by dramatic skits, songs, and improvisations, has produced accelerated learning that is sustained over a period of time.[12]

As arts programs are being deleted from schools around the country because of budget problems, cognitive development may be suffering. For example, in the alternative Magnet Arts Elementary School in Eugene, Oregon, the arts are incorporated in the total program. Reading and writing are taught through playwriting and acting. Dance is used in math instruction; science students make musical instruments. In 1976, the Magnet Arts School's sixth graders tied for first place in reading and fifth place in math among the district's 30 schools.[13]

According to Don L. Brigham, "'Visual preference' students are often considered slow learners, but they can learn through a program that recognizes their needs, which are different from those of their verbal-analytical classmates."[14]

In *Coming to Our Senses,* members of the Arts Education and Americans Panel wrote that:

The arts provide unique ways of knowing about the world and should be central to learning for this reason alone. But it is also significant that art education can influence two elements of human behavior which concern every teacher: discipline and motivation. Art requires tremendous discipline. . . . Learning an art is learning to care passionately about tiny details as well as overall excellence. On the other hand, the arts can bring enormous pleasure; all of us are motivated to do what brings pleasure. A successful art experience motiviates the child to look further and deeper.[15]

Initiating, Developing, and Evaluating a Program of Interdisciplinary Arts

Administrators, teachers, or community members wishing to provide interdisciplinary art experiences in their schools must look at three areas: (1) initiating the program; (2) developing curriculum and teaching strategies; and (3) evaluating the procedure and the results. The adjustments necessary to the success of an interdisciplinary approach cost little money, but they require a concern for the value of the arts and a commitment to maintain the arts as a vital part of the curriculum and the lives of students.

The administrator is the key individual in each aspect, leading the staff and the community in valuing the arts as basic components of education. Although not every teacher will present actual instruction in the arts, the administrator must help all teachers to cultivate a cooperative attitude and demonstrate a willingness to foster the arts in education.

The idea of a curriculum in which the arts are allowed equity with other subjects is persistent and currently receiving increasing attention as school districts look beyond traditional basics toward a balanced education. Recognizing both the constraints and

---

[11]Earl J. Ogletree, "Curriculum for Two Modes of Consciousness," *Contemporary Education,* Vol. 49 (summer, 1978), 205.

[12]Sheila Ostrander and Lynn Schroeder, *Superlearning.* New York: Delacorte Publishing Co., 1979, p. 31.

[13]Roger M. Williams, "Why Children Should Draw: The Surprising Link Between Art and Learning," *The Saturday Review,* Vol. 4 (September 3, 1977), 14-15.

[14]Don L. Brigham, "Art and Learning: Partners in Educational Process," *Studies in Art Education,* Vol. 19, No. 3 (1978), 25.

[15]*Coming to Our Senses: The Significance of the Arts for American Education.* Arts, Education and Americans Panel. New York: McGraw-Hill Book Co., 1977, pp. 6-7. Used by permission of the publisher.

the possibilities of venturing into an interdisciplinary arts program is important.

Time is important in two ways: It takes time to plan and institute an arts-in-education curriculum. Building support for the idea, overcoming inertia and turning to new directions, changing old, individualistic ways of teaching to new, cooperative methods—all this takes time. Time is also needed to give the arts their share of minutes per week, or hours per semester.

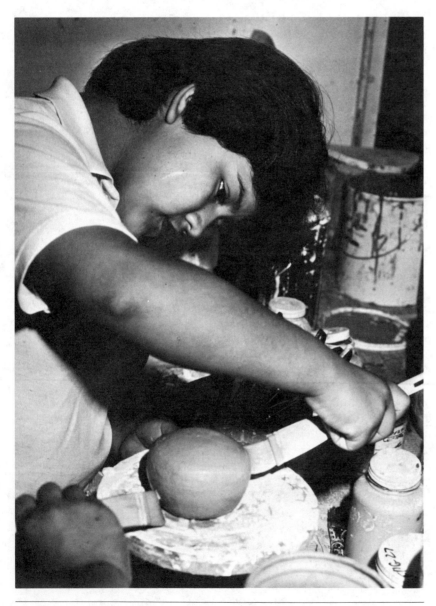

Research must be done to avoid "reinventing the wheel." That means reviewing the literature, writing to sites beyond the local area, and visiting existing models whenever possible.

The content has possibilities limited only by the choices and decisions of the curriculum planners. Such decisions depend on the amount of information gathered and understanding attained.

Fundamental to these content decisions is a survey or needs assessment to determine the gap between what exists and what is the desired goal. Such an appraisal must be realistic, based on facts rather than assumptions.

Staff development is a critical area. Most teachers will need to make some accommodation to the new program; others will have to make major modifications in their goals, their skills, and their ways of working. Staff relationships must be developed toward a sharing mode, and then ideas can be introduced, reinforced, and enhanced.

Evaluation needs to be an important part of the instructional plan, including assessment at many predetermined periods. It should be concerned with a spectrum of aspects of the program, including curriculum design, the talents and proficiencies of the staff, strategies of teaching, the adequacy of the physical plant, the quality and suitability of materials and equipment, the degree of support from the community, and of course, the level of student progress and satisfaction. Evaluation must be broader than checklists and paper-and-pencil tests to include such techniques as observation and interviews with staff and students. It needs to be conducted by knowledgeable, sensitive people with a concern for the balanced education of students toward their informed, responsible, and caring citizenship.

Chapter 7

Program Development

Developing a quality program in the arts depends on a number of program components: qualified personnel, administrative and community support, adequate facilities and equipment, a broad-based curriculum, a long-range district plan, and ongoing program evaluation.

Qualified Personnel

The success of any program to educate children and youths depends on competent teachers. This is an ongoing process which includes preservice education; careful selection of adequately prepared classroom teachers, specialists, and consultants; and a quality program of continuing education and staff development.

Preservice Education

Colleges, universities, and school districts need to have a closer coalition in improving teacher education in the arts. This would make possible realistic and early contact between potential teachers and the field. This is important because student teaching under qualified master teachers continues to be the most productive single experience in teacher preparation. Therefore, internships during the entire educational program, as business majors now have, should be fostered. This concept could strengthen the education of teachers of the arts as well as provide additional art expertise in the field.

Because of the importance of multi-arts experiences in early childhood education and the lack of background in the arts of most classroom teachers in California, an emphasis in the arts should be an option in elementary teacher education programs. A background in the arts would be essential to qualify an individual for this option. This approach would be a means of providing competent arts educators for early childhood education programs or elementary schools, which do not have the benefit of specialists as an avenue for upgrading their arts programs. Because these teachers would have a general elementary credential, they could be hired in the primary grades or in a small elementary school as a regular classroom teacher. In addition, they could serve as consultants in the arts or as an arts specialist in a teaching team.

Qualifications in the Arts for Classroom Teachers

Every teacher should have an understanding and appreciation of the arts and be able to use art forms effectively in the classroom. The teacher who uses the total environment and a multisensory approach to all subject matter creates in the child an excitement and fresh outlook towards the learning process. The classroom teacher should also be able to create an atmosphere that allows students to express their individual perceptions as they experiment with and internalize new ideas and creative ways to communicate their experiences through the arts.

Qualifications for Arts Specialists/Consultants

Ideally, the arts specialists/consultants should possess a thorough knowledge of the interrelationship of all the arts in addition to an in-depth specialization in one or more areas. A commitment to the arts process as well as a cultural and humanistic understanding of the arts is important. An appreciation of and respect for the aesthetic experiences derived from the arts are also essential. Special qualifications exist for the arts specialist at the early childhood, intermediate, and secondary levels in each area.

The teacher of the arts in early childhood education should possess:

- Special interest in the arts
- Belief in the importance of the arts experience
- Comprehension of the learning processes as they relate to the arts and the maturation of children

- Competence in working with young children in the arts
- Experience in all of the arts, with a specialization in at least one of the arts or have a multiarts emphasis

The specialist of the arts in the middle school should also have the above qualifications, except that the last mentioned specialization should be demonstrated in terms of a major or minor in one of the arts. The following qualifications are also necessary at this level:

- Knowledge of methodology in arts literature, criticism, history, and aesthetics
- Ability and interest in the utilization of community resources

At the secondary level a specialist in one of the arts, in addition to attainment of the above listed qualifications, should have:

- A major in one of the arts
- A minor, or related courses, in one or more of the other arts

Each teacher of the arts, in relating to learners in the classroom, should be able to:

- Teach the arts developmentally.
- Understand and apply arts concepts.
- Relate the arts to other subject areas.
- Use appropriate arts vocabulary.
- Write and talk about the arts and artists.
- Obtain materials through many sources.
- Feel comfortable in expressing self in the arts.
- Have a knowledge of aesthetics, methodology, and history of the arts.

Continuing Education and Staff Development for Teachers

Continuing professional growth is essential for all teachers. Professional development in the arts is particularly important for the classroom teacher who has the responsibility to teach the arts. This is a crucial concern because most classroom teachers have inadequate training in the arts. The responsibility of providing the staff development of teachers falls on county offices, school districts, administrators, and arts specialists/consultants. Teachers should be encouraged to enroll in arts courses in local colleges, universities, or special workshops and also to seek the help of county offices, community service organizations, and national organizations. In addition, arts teachers should assume the professional responsibility of keeping current in their fields by visiting art galleries and museums; attending concerts, the theatre, and dance programs; and participating in other related arts experiences.

Resources for obtaining further education tend to be the same as for any other teachers: professional development programs (conferences, workshops, seminars, and the like), staff meetings with emphasis on instructional concerns, professional library resources, arts-related work experience, travel with an arts emphasis, and any other experiences that can be used to enhance a teacher's background in the arts. Attending exhibits and performances is one resource not relevant to teachers in many other areas, but it is of prime importance to the teacher of the arts.

Administrative and Community Support

The key to building successful programs in the arts is enthusiastic and realistic support at all levels of the school community—from parents to district administrators.

Arts Consultants

Since not all teachers are adequately prepared to use the arts in the classroom effectively, each school district should have the resource of qualified certificated arts consultants either at the district or the county level. Arts consultants provide teachers with experiences, strategies, and insights into the affective, aesthetic, and nonverbal elements of arts education. The arts consultant should be used to focus, motivate, coordinate, and supplement the conduct of arts programs.

Arts consultants cannot function effectively in isolation. Close relationships must be established with the entire school community. Through such relationships, the arts can evolve as an integral part of the school curriculum for all students and can have a significant influence on the general philosophy of teaching in that community.

To be effective, the consultants must:

- Be knowledgeable in all areas of the arts for which they are responsible.
- Understand learning patterns and the physical capabilities of various age levels.
- Become part of the school family by expanding concerns beyond the limits of the arts program.
- Establish a working relationship with other arts consultants and arts teachers.
- Schedule regular periods of work with classroom teachers to further their understanding of the intent and value of the arts, the relationships of the arts, and the ways in which the arts can be integrated into the general curriculum.
- Present the arts in such a way that the nonartist may intelligently and comfortably use the arts media in the classroom.
- Encourage classroom teachers to work within the realm of their own style and personality; to be able to cope with realities of their situations; (e.g., available space, accompaniment, time, temperament, and size of class); and to learn to evaluate the work of their students.

Administrative Responsibilities

Administrators, school district boards of education, and offices of county superintendents of schools can use this framework as the basis for the adoption, development, and implementation of arts curricula to meet the needs of the students in local communities. These responsibilities can be met by taking the following steps:

- Support the allotment of a minimum of time with the arts each week on a consistent and sequential base, with maximum use of the student's time at the elementary level.
- Encourage a requirement of a minimum of one year in the arts for high school graduation.
- Provide qualified instructional personnel who will conduct the program and develop procedures for maintaining professional competence.
- Adopt instructional resource materials and teaching strategies to support and enrich classroom studies, including essential instructional aids, such as books, audiovisual materials, and teacher references as well as typical arts materials, tools, and equipment.
- Develop objectives for local arts programs and curriculum guides designed to meet local needs.
- Provide for ongoing evaluation, review, and improvement of arts programs, again involving cross-sectional committees and individual teachers in evaluation, design, and developmental activities.
- Establish local arts advisory and support groups to aid in curriculum planning and in the implementation of the arts programs. Such groups should include representative teachers, students, and principals, and, when possible, community representatives, practicing artists, professional evaluators, and members of professional curriculum staffs.

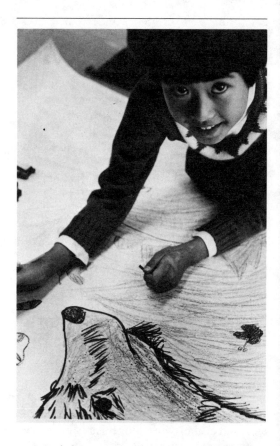

Administrators should be aware of the arts as a special tool for enriching the entire curriculum. Many programs across the nation have provided dramatic evidence of the capacity of arts education programs to contribute to overall improvement in a student's academic achievement. Development of arts programs and their implementation can help to meet the needs of the total curriculum.

Scheduling

Arts program planners should consider the diverse possibilities for scheduling effective arts education programs, keeping in view the time available to all within the regular elementary school day. Modular scheduling and other flexible plans often provide desirable alternatives. Provisions should allow for instruction to take place in small-group as well as in large-group situations.

At the secondary level, the daily schedule should include a number of arts course offerings. Careful planning should prevent program conflicts as much as possible so that students are not forced to eliminate arts classes for scheduling reasons alone.

Financial Support

Programs in the arts should be supported at a priority level equal to that of other curriculum areas within the regular district and school budget allocations. Consideration should be given to needs unique to each program, such as specially trained personnel and special materials, supplies, equipment, space, classrooms, and studio facilities. In addition, staff development is part of curriculum planning and must be considered in making the arts an integral part of the curriculum.

Community Resources

School districts should seek the cooperation of community art agencies, local colleges and universities, museums, and individual artists who are willing to provide services to schools to promote school program goals. Communication should always be two-way among and with such groups. Some ways in which these human and physical resources can be utilized include the use of an artist-in-residence to visit certain schools on regular schedules to spark or enrich an arts program, field trips for students to participate in experiences not brought to schools, and artists and touring groups visiting the school.

Adequate Facilities and Equipment for the Arts

The quality of programs in the arts will be proportional to the adequacy and appropriateness of the physical facilities available to accommodate the type and scope of arts programs being offered. For example, consideration must be given to free space for activities requiring movement, wooden floors for dance, provisions for clean-up after art experiences, and

acoustical treatment of rooms for musical ensembles.

It is also important that districts and schools select quality materials and equipment which will effectively support the goals and objectives of their arts education programs. In making these selections, standards that reflect the specialized needs of each of the arts must be considered. Classroom teachers and arts specialists should be consulted in developing these standards.

A Broad-based Curriculum

The curriculum should be broad enough to meet the needs of all students as well as to provide for special interests and populations.

Career Education

Accelerating change has had an undeniable impact on society and technology. Schools must recognize these changes and the implications they hold for life career planning. In recent years young people have adopted career choices to fit opportunities that were nonexistent in previous years. Many of these opportunities have occurred within the arts fields.

Career education programs have started to develop before the secondary school level. Programs are now being initiated at the elementary school level as well as the junior/intermediate and senior high school levels. Arts programs should reflect these trends and provide career information which can be integrated into a student's elementary and junior high school experiences. These experiences should be in addition to the opportunities made available to senior high school students.

Definitive information to assist schools in planning for quality career education courses and programs is available from various sources (see the selected references for each discipline in this framework, Appendix B).

Multicultural Concerns

Teachers of the arts need training and experience in understanding children of diverse cultural backgrounds. They can relate appropriately to a multicultural, democratic society by demonstrating receptiveness toward viewpoints or artistic products from different cultures. Such demonstrations, based on diverse criteria, include encouraging artistic expression that reflects characteristics and aesthetic values from divergent cultures and providing opportunities and a supportive environment for students to experience quality artistic products related to various cultures.

Gifted and Talented Students

Identified gifted students have talents that can contribute to the future well-being of society if developed to their fullest. This group provides the potential leaders, the creative thinkers, the achievers, the artists, the scientists, and the brain trusts for the future. For their own well-being and also for the well-being of society, these children need to be physically and mentally healthy and balanced human beings. The arts are basic to the education of a fully functioning human being; therefore, it is important that the gifted also have a balanced curriculum which includes the arts.

Artistically gifted students who show high-level ability in the expressive, critical, or historical aspects of the arts must be encouraged to pursue the development of such strengths. For these students, appropriate intensive work in the arts should be arranged.

Special Education

Creative experiences can be instrumental in providing beauty and joy to students with mental, physical, or learning disabilities. The arts open the senses and expand awareness by enriching even a limited environment.

Self-concept is particularly important for special students. The arts provide students additional avenues for achieving success. It is possible to increase feelings of self-worth for these students by developing alternative forms of communication and channels to express feelings and ideas in a variety of learning modes through the arts.

The arts fulfill an important function in reinforcing learning for these students. However, it is also essential that the arts be included in their curriculum to develop other talents that they may possess. The arts can help all children know that they are unique and special.

A District Plan for the Arts

To restore the proper balance in the curriculum and provide adequate programs in the arts, districts need to initiate a long-range plan for the arts. This plan should include:

- A proposed curriculum for the arts based on this framework
- Allotment of adequate time in the school program

- A staffing plan
- A survey of facilities and equipment to determine what is needed
- A survey of community resources
- An estimate of financial support needed
- A recommendation for realizing the plan
- A continuing assessment to ensure that the plan *is* being followed

Program Evaluation

When evaluating arts programs, one makes reference to the broader scope of evaluation, rather than to the assessment of performance objectives. For this broader scope, the following aspects of all arts programs should be considered: program characteristics, program implementation, and program effects.

Program characteristics are based on these factors:

- Curriculum
  1. Overall goals and objectives
  2. Curriculum guides
  3. Sequential instructions in each of the arts meeting goals and objectives
  4. Interdisciplinary concepts
- Environmental conditions
  1. Special facilities
  2. Special equipment
  3. Human climate
- Target populations
  1. General students
  2. Special students
  3. Gifted and talented students
  4. Multicultural students

Program implementation is composed of these aspects:

- Staff development
- Data collection
  1. For crediting accomplishments
  2. For future planning
- Instructional resources
- Scheduling

Program effect includes:

- Effect on individuals
- Impact on the community
- Contribution of the arts to other subject areas
- Contribution of the arts to multicultural understanding

Gathering the data necessary to make judgments about all these aspects of a program will require the development of instruments of varying kinds, including questionnaires, observation schedules, informal teacher assessments, and criterion-referenced tests. These instruments will need to be referenced to different levels of responsibility, such as the district, the school, and the individual classroom.

To carry out this broad program evaluation, properly qualified experts should make judgments about arts programs. In many cases this approach may mean seeking outside consultants to augment staff resources available within the district. As these alternative viewpoints are brought to bear on the program, a more comprehensive and objective base will become available for those making program decisions.

A Final Note

This framework is dedicated to the child of the twenty-first century who needs to be:

- Flexible
- Self-disciplined
- Self-reliant
- Creative
- Imaginative
- Perceptive
- Self-confident
- Self-motivated
- Adaptable
- Responsible
- Appreciative

The curriculum that has been recommended here will prepare students to cope with the rapidly changing aspects of a technologically oriented world.

Criteria
for Evaluating
Instructional
Materials

Criteria for Evaluating Instructional Materials in Music

Kindergarten Through Grade Eight

Approved by the California State Board of Education on March 9, 1978

I. Introduction

The criteria for evaluating instructional materials in music shall reflect the philosophy expressed in the *Visual and Performing Arts Framework*. The primary objective of the music curriculum should be to develop the ability of every child to perceive and respond to the aesthetic content of music. Consequently, a series of music textbooks should be judged according to the excellence of their musical content and the systematic contribution that this content will make to a total program of music education. The necessity for quality in a series of music textbooks is paramount. The following is an outline of suggested criteria for evaluating music materials:

II. Quality of Music

A. Musical selections should generally include melodies of expressive quality. Books in a series should generally contain numerous examples of each of several characteristic melodic structures; i.e., patterns that move scalewise, chordwise, by repeated tones, or in sequence. In books for upper grades, the inclusion of songs using a 12-tone row and melodies using such devices as inversion, augmentation, and diminution is desirable.

B. The voice parts in part songs shall be "singable," and the range of difficulty of the songs shall be varied. The accompaniment to each song, whether played on the piano or on other instruments, shall be appropriate to the melodic style and period of the song. All accompaniments shall conform to generally accepted principles of harmony, whether traditional or contemporary.

C. The rhythm of each melody and the verbal pattern of the text shall conform to each other artistically. Accented beats of the measure and accented words or syllables shall normally coincide. In pupils' books, rhythmic structures so difficult as to require rote learning shall be avoided. In general the rhythmic notation of songs shall be comprehensible to the children who will use the books.

D. Each song book should contain many songs in which the musical relationships among phrases are so precisely defined that children can readily recognize them and thereby discover the musical form. Recognition of design is essential to the understanding of music.

E. Songs and their voice parts shall be within the voice range of the majority of the pupils for whom they are intended.

F. The instrumental compositions and songs included in the books shall be of excellent quality and of various types. There shall be a balance between folk songs and songs by significant composers of the past and present. Folk songs shall be representative not only of various countries but also of various regions of the United States. Books shall include songs and compositions for listening that represent a variety of ethnic groups.

III. Quality of Texts

A. The text of each song shall possess intrinsic merit and be suitable to the grade level for which it is intended.

B. Each song book should generally include some songs in their original languages with phonetic indications of correct *pronunciations*. Translations of these songs in poetic or prose form shall be included in books for pupils and teachers. Translations may also be used as texts of songs if they possess poetic quality, are appropriate in content for the age level involved, and conform to the music.

C. Translated texts of songs shall be as faithful as possible to the original text.

D. Songs containing dialect offensive to any ethnic group are not acceptable.

IV. Music Listening Selections

A. Books for pupils should generally contain some material that will encourage them to listen for specific features of songs and instrumental compositions. In like manner, materials for teachers shall include detailed suggestions to aid them in developing the ability of children to listen to music intelligently and to understand and enjoy it.

B. Composition included in the textbooks for listening purposes shall represent a variety of performance media and contrasting styles and periods and shall be related to the sequential development of concepts.

C. Books for pupils should generally include themes of musical compositions recommended for listening and shall provide authentic background material on the music itself and its composer. Materials for teachers should include additional information designed to assist them in promoting the children's understanding and appreciation of the music selected for listening.

D. Materials for grades seven and eight shall emphasize music listening activities through which young people will be guided to discover for themselves the meaning and structure of music. It is desirable that some material be included that will emphasize not only vocal and instrumental performance but composing and conducting activities as well.

E. Textbooks shall provide a variety of materials supportive of varied activities, such as playing instruments, reading rhythmic scores, and singing (physical as well as mental activities).

V. Organization of Material

The content of each book and of each series as a whole shall be set forth in a manner that will clearly provide for a sequential program of instruction. The program shall contribute to children's understanding of the nature, meaning, and structure of music and to the development of concepts of rhythm, melody, harmony, form, tempo, dynamics, and tone color.

VI. Type of Content

A. Books should generally contain an adequate amount of each of the following types of material: folk, art, and seasonal songs; songs expressive of moral and spiritual values; and songs of a patriotic and historical nature. For middle and upper grades, occasional selections from light operas, operas, and oratorios appropriate to the grade level are desirable. Textbooks shall include songs by contemporary composers, especially those of the United States. Songs of various ethnic origins should be included.

B. Materials for pupils and teachers shall include information that will promote understanding of the cultural significance and expressive meanings of songs.

C. Books for pupils should contain some material organized systematically to promote understanding of the meaning of symbols of musical notation and skill in using them. Books for teachers shall include clearly stated directions for implementing this program.

D. Rounds, canons, descants, and chants are desirable at all grade levels. In books for middle grades, simple two-part songs are desirable. Books for upper grades shall include some unison songs and a considerable amount of material in two and three parts.

E. Vocal music for grades seven and eight shall include examples of two-, three-, and four-part songs (SA, SSA, SAT, SAB, and SATB).

F. In books for grades five through eight, some songs shall contain the melody in parts other than the soprano. It is particularly important that some songs in books for grades seven and eight have the melody written in the bass clef in a range that will be comfortable for boys with changing or changed voices.

G. The notation of music in pupils' and teachers' editions at all levels shall include authentic indications of such expressive elements as tempo and dynamics.

H. The content of books and other instructional materials shall provide for the listening program to such an extent that it is balanced in importance and significance with performance (both vocal and instrumental), improvisation, composing, and conducting.

I. Books shall provide for musical experiences of intrinsic value organized to promote a sequential development of skill in reading and writing music. These musical experiences shall also contribute to the reinforcement of previous learnings.

VII. Instrumental Activities

A. Materials for each grade shall include some songs that suggest the use of instruments, such as the autoharp, bells, the recorder or other flutelike instruments, and percussion and orchestral instruments. In books for pupils, the notation of instrumental parts to be played by children shall be included when appropriate.

B. All textbooks shall contain indications of the correct chords for songs that may appropriately be accompanied by autoharp or other chordal instruments. Any indication of chords must be consistent with the key in which the song is notated. In both pupils' and teachers' editions, the notation of appropriate rhythm patterns for some accompaniments shall be included.

C. For middle and upper grades, materials for pupils shall contain some songs scored in a manner that will facilitate the playing of orchestral instruments by children. The orchestrations shall be interesting melodically and rhythmically.

D. Textbooks or other materials shall include a representation of the relationship of the piano keyboard to the musical staff. The drawing of the staff shall be large and shall be placed above the pictured keyboard. An illustration of the autoharp shall also be provided.

E. When material directly related to an instrument or group of instruments is presented, appropriate illustrations and factual information shall also be given. The illustrations shall be authentic and shall depict the relative sizes of instruments within a given family. It is desirable, whenever possible, that pictures of the instruments be related to those used in the recordings.

F. In books for middle and upper grades, there shall be at least one reproduction of a page from a full orchestral score that is related to the music the children are studying, along with a brief explanation of the score's most important features. An illustration of a symphony orchestra accompanied by a seating chart shall be included in the book. Photographs of a concert band

and/or standard chamber music ensembles are also desirable.

VIII. Aids for Teachers

A. Technically superior banded recordings of all songs in each textbook should be available. These recordings should represent a variety of appropriate voice types. The songs should be sung at the appropriate tempo. The words should be understandable. Instrumental accompaniments should be tasteful and authentic and should not overpower the vocal character of the music. The melodic and rhythmic content of the recording should correspond to the score printed in pupils' and teachers' books. When a language other than English is used, those making recordings or tapes should use authentic native or near-native speakers representing male and female adult voices as well as children's voices, using accurate intonation.

B. All recordings of songs and other selections for listening recommended in a series of textbooks must be available for evaluation when the textbooks are being evaluated.

C. The catalog numbers of the records and the page numbers of the recorded songs in the pupils' and teachers' editions shall be cross-referenced and included in the index.

D. Materials for teachers shall include piano accompaniments that are harmonically correct, appropriate to the style of the melody, and playable by some of the pupils or teachers.

E. A teacher's edition of the textbook shall be available to assist the teachers in the effective uses of pupil materials. Pagination shall be the same in both books. Teacher and pupil editions of textbooks within a series must be available for concurrent evaluation.

F. Materials for teachers shall be organized in clearly understandable lesson plans that will help them carry out a sequential program of instruction dealing with the constituent elements of music and their interrelationships.

G. Materials for teachers shall indicate simply and clearly the ways in which they can help children learn to explore music creatively and to investigate and discover the nature, meaning, and structure of music.

H. Textbooks for teachers shall include suggestions for original and exploratory activities for children, including movement to music, through which musical concepts can be developed.

I. Materials for teachers at all grade levels shall provide for musical activities that will contribute to children's development of understandings, attitudes and appreciations, and skills.

J. An appendix listing available visual aids, supplementary recordings, programmed learning materials, and resource books is desirable.

IX. Physical Features

The following aspects of format and other physical features of books shall conform to acceptable standards:

A. The general appearance of the textbooks shall be appealing to children.

B. Both the text and the musical notation shall be clear and easy to read.

C. In part songs included in books for grades four through eight, the notation of the individual parts shall be clearly defined and easy to read. Many of the part songs shall be notated, with each part on a separate staff.

D. Bindings shall be strong and durable and shall permit the book to remain flat when open. Bindings must not obscure inner margins.

E. An attractive cover design is desirable.

F. Whenever possible, the songs shall be spaced on the page so that the phrase structure is easily apparent, with no phrase broken between two lines.

G. Each book should be attractively illustrated to stimulate children's interest in the music and to enhance the music's mood and spirit. These illustrations shall not interfere with the musical notation presented.

H. Illustrations of children participating in activities related to the music shall reflect the multiethnic composition of our society.

I. The materials in textbooks for pupils and teachers shall be indexed alphabetically and shall also be classified as to topics and types of music. In teachers' editions there shall be an additional classification of materials in terms of elements of music, leading toward the development of concepts. In the classified index, both the title of each song and the number of the page on which it occurs shall be cited. Each song included in the textbook for pupils shall be presented on the corresponding page in the teacher's edition. The organization of the indexes shall be consistent among all books in a given series.

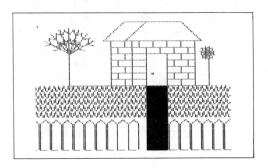

Addenda to Criteria for Evaluating Instructional Materials in Music

I. Criteria for Evaluating Supplementary Materials

A. Instrumental Music

Materials should promote a sequential development of skills in pupils.

1. Materials should include selections for a variety of standard band and/or orchestral instruments.
2. Simple performance music suitable to each ability level of the student should be included and graded as to difficulty.
3. A section on the care and maintenance of instruments should be included at each level.
4. Clearly illustrated fingering charts should be included at each level.
5. Materials for the recorder should indicate fingerings in both baroque and German.
6. Illustrations of proper playing posture are desirable.
7. Instrumentation and number of parts should reflect the prevailing instrumentation of the average elementary, middle, and/or junior high school; e.g., large numbers of trumpets, clarinets, and flutes.
8. Wherever possible, parts should be divided in such a manner that beginners are able to perform with more advanced players.
9. It is desirable to have inexpensive recordings accompany the materials.

B. Choral Music

1. Whenever possible, collections of songs, unison, part songs, part songs with descants, and partner songs are desirable.
2. Choral music that reflects the ethnic and cultural diversity of the society should be encouraged.
3. Lyrics and style should be appropriate for the level submitted.

II. Criteria for Evaluating Religious Content in Materials

Any materials of a religious nature in instructional materials will have been evaluated first for compliance with Education Code sections 60044(a) and (b). However, if instructional materials contain any discussion, depiction, or other aspect of religion, they shall also be evaluated to meet the following educational criteria:

A. Materials commonly recognized as having sectarian religious content should be treated in instructional materials in ways that contribute to the understanding of musical style and musical history, to the development of musical concepts and skills, and to the recognition of music as an element of cultural diversity.

B. Songs commonly recognized as having sectarian religious content shall be included in basic materials, both in quantity and placement, only as required to achieve a specified educational purpose.

C. Materials for teachers shall contain suggestions that will assist the teacher in recognizing the religious diversity of students in the classroom and in being sensitive to feelings that children may have when asked to participate in singing songs that are not of their own religious background.

D. Materials for teachers should provide ample information or instruction on how to present religious songs in such a way as to comply with legal constraints.

E. Teacher and student materials shall not contain directions or suggest activities for students that could be considered adorational or devotional in nature and that may require students to participate in any religious observance.

F. Except where a material deals with a specific nationality or a partic- ular social, ethnic, or cultural group or a particular historical era in the United States or California, music materials should reflect the religious diversity in contemporary and historical United States' society.

G. Any materials which are used to describe particular religious practices should refer to the generic group which observes such practices. Thus, except as it may appear in lyrics, the pronoun *we* should not be used in reference to any cultural or religious group.

Criteria for Evaluating Instructional Materials in Art

Kindergarten Through Grade Eight

Approved by the California State Board of Education
December 14, 1978

I. Introduction

The criteria for evaluating instructional materials in art shall reflect the philosophy expressed in the *Visual and Performing Arts Framework*.

The four major goals of art education are the development of (1) visual and tactile perception; (2) skills of creative expression; (3) knowledge or art heritage; and (4) bases for aesthetic judgment.

1. *Visual and Tactile Perception* heightens students' awareness and sensitivity to the world about them. Perception is developed as students see, feel, and understand form, color, and texture as well as visual subtleties in daily experiences. The ability to perceive is fundamental to art expression and appreciation.

2. *Creative and Expressive Skills* are developed through direct personal experiences with art materials. Art instruction is designed to enable students to communicate ideas and feelings, as well as images and symbols in visual forms.

3. *Art Heritage* study includes investigating historical, contemporary and popular art, fine art, and folk art. It is essential for students to understand that art has a past and a present and that it has always been an important part of the lives of people everywhere. Knowledge of the arts is an important way for students to understand the cultural heritage and values of different ethnic and cultural groups.

4. *Aesthetic Judgment* involves the study of visual, intellectual, and philosophic bases for understanding art and for making judgements about its form, content, technique, and purpose. As a result, students learn to identify issues and to develop criteria for appraising visual forms and arriving at personal preferences and opinions. Concern for the quality of the visual environment is increased as aesthetic judgment is developed.

Instructional materials may address one or more of these goals as appropriate.

II. Student Materials

A variety of instructional materials, including books, films, videotapes and cassettes, filmstrips, illustrations, reproductions, slides, transparencies, manipulative materials, and learning games will be considered.

Student materials shall:

1. Demonstrate to the student that art is a means to enrich the quality of daily life.

2. Include works which promote students' understanding of the intent and aesthetic quality of the art form, drawing upon a range of subject matter representative of all aspects of life, such as human forms, historical, political, and social events.

3. Include art processes and techniques which stimulate students' ideas and personal imagery and not merely present methods for making products.

4. Present art works from major periods of history which are

representative of art throughout the world.

5. Encourage the use of a variety of art media and materials for creative expression, such as drawing, painting, sculpture, graphics, ceramics, crafts, fibers, photography, film, and video.

6. Heighten the students' sensitivity to the environment by providing activities to increase their knowledge as well as to extend and strengthen their visual and tactile awareness.

7. Be appropriate for the age of the student.

8. Provide a continuum of experiences from simple to complex.

9. Provide for differences in learning styles, interests, and aptitudes.

10. Introduce new terms and develop and expand the students' art vocabulary.

11. Present discussion topics and follow-up activities which contribute to the students' understanding of:

   a. The structure of art: elements (form, color, texture, line) and principles of design

   b. The meaning of art: origins, content, influences, purposes

   c. The relevance of art to the individual and to society

12. Develop awareness of local and national resources, such as museums, galleries, and collections which provide opportunities to view original works of art.

13. Relate art to other arts disciplines and subject areas.

14. Present information about art careers and related vocations.

15. Include suggestions for ongoing self-evaluation.

16. Include brand names, commercial representations, and logos only when such examples are clearly related to instructional purposes.

17. Treat examples of art depicting religious subjects in ways that contribute to the understanding of art and art history, to the development of art concepts and skills, and to the recognition of art as an element of culture.

18. Unless specifically dealing with a limited cultural topic or historical period, include information about the artistic contributions of all groups within the United States: Asians, Blacks, Europeans, Native Americans, Latins, and other ethnic and cultural groups, identifying the expressive characteristics of their art forms. Materials will also represent various socioeconomic and geographic groups, ages, and sexes.

III. Teacher Materials

Materials should provide teaching strategies for perceptual development, for exploring the historical and cultural background of art, for producing art, for examining art, for talking and reading about art, and for evaluating student progress in art.

Teacher materials shall:

1. Suggest specific ways in which the teacher can provide leadership and guidance to help children develop understanding and appreciation of art and skills for perceiving and creating art.

2. Include examples of clearly understandable lesson plans, organized in a sequential order of instruction, with multiple points of entry.

3. Suggest teaching strategies which provide for differences in learning styles, interests, aptitudes, and achievement.

4. Include information, discussion topics, and follow-up enrichment activities.
5. Include suggestions for organizing learning experiences for individual, small, and large group activities.
6. Provide sufficient teacher information to be usable by teachers with limited art background.
7. Provide current bibliographies and listings of related instructional materials and suggestions for their use.
8. Indicate various ways in which art may be related to other subject areas.
9. Include suggestions for formal and informal techniques for evaluation of student progress, such as performance and verbal assessments, observation techniques, individual inventories, skill development reviews, checklists, and standardized and teacher-designed tests.
10. Contain information about child growth and development in art.

Selected References

Dance Selected References

Arnheim, Daniel. *Dance Injuries: Their Prevention and Care.* Pennington, N.J.: Princeton Book Company, 1987.

One of the first books to deal with prevention and care of a dancer's injuries.

Blom, Lynn A., and L. Tarin Chaplin. *The Intimate Act of Choreography.* Pittsburgh: University of Pittsburgh Press, 1982.

An approach to the creative process applicable for beginning to advanced students in choreography. Improvisational ideas included.

Children's Dance (Revised edition). Reston, Va.: American Alliance for Health, Physical Education, Recreation and Dance Staff, 1981.

NOTE: The references contained in this section are representative of the many recent publications available for each of the arts disciplines. The references have not been endorsed by the California State Board of Education or the State Department of Education's Curriculum Development and Supplemental Materials Commission, and no official endorsement should be inferred. All entries were submitted by leaders in visual and performing arts education in California.

Designed to show how dance can be used in the classroom in lively, innovative ways. Appropriate for the classroom teacher as well as the specialist in dance and physical activities. Covers such topics as dance as an expression of feelings, folk and ethnic contributions, dancing for boys, and dance composition.

Jacob, Ellen. *Dancing: A Guide for the Dancer You Can Be* (Fourth edition). New York: Danceway Books, n.d.

Covers a broad range of topics from what to wear for dance class to how to warm up. Definitions of dance styles included. A resource book for teachers and for upper elementary through high school students.

Jowitt, Deborah. *The Dance in Mind: Profiles and Reviews, 1977–83.* Boston: Godine, 1985.

Reviews and reflects on modern and postmodern dance artists and performances in New York City.

Joyce, Mary. *Dance Technique for Children.* Mountain View, Calif.: Mayfield Publishing Company, n.d.

A description of dance techniques for children. Provides a technical support system to teachers working from a creative approach with upper elementary and middle school students.

Kraus, Richard, and Sarah Charman. *A History of the Dance in Art and Education* (Second edition). Englewood Cliffs, N.J.: Prentice Hall, 1981.

Traces development of modern dance and classical ballet in America. Explains dance styles, the work of important choreographers, and the place of dance in education at the high school and college levels.

Martin, John. *Modern Dance*. Pennington, N.J.: Princeton Book Company, n.d.

An aesthetic philosophical statement about modern dance in the United States. Provides a view of dance in the 1930s and 1940s.

Mazo, Joseph H. *Prime Movers: The Makers of Modern Dance in America*. Pennington, N.J.: Princeton Book Company, 1983.

Describes major figures in modern dance during the 1960s and 1970s. Presents useful photographs that capture the period.

Sherbon, Elizabeth. *On the Count of One: Modern Dance Methods* (Third edition). Mountain View, Calif.: Mayfield Publishing Company, 1985.

Describes modern dance methods for movement education.

Turner, Margery J. *New Dance: Approaches to Nonliteral Choreography*. Pittsburgh: University of Pittsburgh Press, 1976.

A complete guide to defining and teaching nonliteral dance. Sample lessons provided throughout.

Weikart, Phyllis S. *Teaching Movement and Dance*. Ypsilanti, Mich.: High/Scope Educational Research Foundation, High-Scope Press, 1982.

Provides a sequential approach to teaching rhythmic movement.

Drama/Theatre Selected References

Albright, Hardie, and Arnita Albright. *Acting: The Creative Process* (Third edition). Belmont, Calif.: Wadsworth Publishing Company, 1980.

A basic acting text intended for high school drama classes.

Coger, Leslie I., and Melvin R. White. *Readers Theatre Handbook* (Third edition). Glenview, Ill.: Scott, Foresman & Company, 1982.

Techniques given for adapting, rehearsing, and staging group interpretations of narrative literature.

Corson, Richard. *Stage Makeup* (Seventh edition). Englewood Cliffs, N.J.: Prentice Hall, 1986.

Includes 400 illustrations, 23 plates of period hairstyles, and color charts of step-by-step procedures in theatrical makeup.

Dietrich, John, and Ralph Duckwall. *Play Direction* (Second edition). Englewood Cliffs, N.J.: Prentice Hall, 1983.

Describes script selection and analysis, preparation for rehearsal, and steps for guiding actors through the process.

Latshaw, George. *The Theatre Student and Puppetry: The Ultimate Disguise*. New York: Rosen Publishing Group, 1978.

Numerous ideas presented for designing, constructing, and using puppets in dramatic expression and performance.

McCaslin, Nellie. *Creative Drama in the Intermediate Grades*. White Plains, N.Y.: Longman Group USA, 1987.

Introduction to the philosophy and practice of using improvisational drama to introduce drama as an art form and as a teaching strategy in other content areas. Presents ideas for lesson planning and suggested materials for upper elementary and early junior high school students to assist teachers without formal training in drama for children.

McCaslin, Nellie. *Creative Drama in the Primary Grades.* White Plains, N.Y.: Longman Group USA, 1987.

Specifically geared to the instructional needs of teachers in the lower elementary grades.

Siks, Geraldine B. *Drama with Children* (Second edition). New York: Harper and Row Publishers, Inc., 1983.

Presents a process-concept approach to introducing the art of drama which complements the drama/theatre component of the *Visual and Performing Arts Framework for California Public Schools.* Suggested lessons and activities given for using drama techniques in other subject matter areas and drama as a means of meeting the needs of special student populations.

Spolin, Viola. *Improvisation for the Theatre: A Handbook of Teaching and Directing Techniques* (Revised edition). Evanston, Ill.: Northwestern University Press, 1983.

Through more than 200 theatre games, demonstrates how a teacher or drama coach can encourage the release of students' inner creativity.

Spolin, Viola. *Theater Games for the Classroom: A Teacher's Handbook.* Evanston, Ill.: Northwestern University Press, 1986.

Contains specific activities and exercises that strengthen the child's sense of play, creativity, imagination, and understanding of basic theatre and drama concepts. Appropriate for kindergarten through grade twelve.

Way, Brian. *Development Through Drama.* Atlantic Highlands, N.J.: Humanities Press International, Inc., 1967.

Useful for teachers in upper elementary grades. Emphasizes the personal development of the child through appreciation for drama as an art. Pro-

vides samples of improvisational exercises and helpful hints for applying drama to social studies instruction.

Music Selected References

Bessom, Malcolm E.; Alphonse M. Tatarunis; and Samuel L. Forcucci. *Teaching Music in Today's Secondary Schools: A Creative Approach to Contemporary Music Education* (Second edition). New York: Harcourt Brace Jovanovich, 1980.

Detailed coverage of the junior and senior high school music curriculum for general music, music listening and music theory, vocal and instrumental music, humanities courses, related arts courses, individualized instruction, and instruction for handicapped and gifted/talented children. Evaluation measures provided.

Choksy, Lois, and others. *Teaching Music in Twentieth-Century America.* Englewood Cliffs, N.J.: Prentice Hall, 1985.

Presents descriptions of four approaches used in North American schools: Jaques, Dalcroze, Orff, and Comprehensive Musicianship. Each approach or method described by a noted authority, and classroom strategies presented.

George, Luvenia A. *Teaching the Music of Six Different Cultures* (Revised edition). Danbury, Conn.: World Music Press, 1988.

Contains an introduction to and an analysis of different kinds of music: African, black American, American Indian, Jewish, Hawaiian, and Puerto Rican. Includes activities for student involvement as well as bibliographic and audiovisual references.

Hackett, Patricia. *The Melody Book.* Englewood Cliffs, N.J.: Prentice Hall, 1983.

Extensive collection of songs from throughout the world. A resource for teachers at all levels.

Hackett, Patricia, and Carolynn Lindeman. *The Musical Classroom* (Second edition). Englewood Cliffs, N.J.: Prentice Hall, 1987.

A resource for elementary teachers. Includes lessons which incorporate both American and European approaches and music of many styles and cultures. One hundred forty-two songs plus instructions for playing five instruments provided.

Harrison, Lois N. *Getting Started in Elementary Music Education*. Englewood Cliffs, N.J.: Prentice Hall, 1983.

Includes concept development related to the elements of music and basic activities for involving children in music.

K–12 Arts Education in the United States: Present Context, Future Needs. Reston, Va.: Music Educators National Conference, 1986.

Source book of contemporary ideas in music education in the United States for the arts education community. Includes a brief history and the current status of music education.

Landis, Beth, and Polly Carder. *The Eclectic Curriculum in American Music Education: Contributions of Dalcroze, Kodaly, and Orff*. Reston, Va.: Music Educators National Conference, 1985.

Describes three prominent European curricular approaches to music education.

Multicultural Perspectives in Music Education. Edited by William Anderson and Patricia Shehan. Reston, Va.: Music Educators National Conference, 1989.

Nash, Grace C. *Creative Approaches to Child Development with Music, Language and Movement: Incorporating the Philosophies and Techniques of Orff, Kodaly, and Laban*. Van Nuys, Calif.: Alfred Publishing Company, Inc., 1974.

Incorporates the philosophies of Orff, Kodaly, and Laban in a classroom approach to music.

Nordoff, Paul, and Clive Robbins. *Music Therapy in Special Education* (Second edition, revised). St. Louis: MMB Music, Inc., 1983.

Describes authors' manner of working with handicapped children of all levels, from completely autistic to trainable.

Olsen, Dale, et al. *Music of Latin America: Mexico, Ecuador, Brazil*. Reston, Va.: Music Educators National Conference, 1987.

Part of a multicultural series originally produced for public radio. Includes three cassettes and a 20-page teacher's guide providing historical and musical background information, pictures of instruments, and suggestions for using the materials with elementary and secondary students. Also includes *Music of Southeast Ansa, Lao, Hmong, and Vietnamese* as part of series.

Randel, Don M. *Harvard Concise Dictionary of Music*. Cambridge, Mass.: Harvard University Press, Belknap Press, 1978.

An authentic source for learning musical terms and vocabulary.

The School Music Program: Description and Standards. Reston, Va.: Music Educators National Conference, 1986.

A resource for school administrators, music educators, and interested parents and citizens concerned about quality programs in music. Describes a music program and provides standards for curriculum, staff, scheduling, facilities, and equipment.

Visual Arts Selected References

Chapman, Laura H. *Instant Art, Instant Culture: The Unspoken Policy for American Schools.* New York: Teachers College, 1982.

A critical commentary on the current status of the visual, performing, and literary arts in our nation's elementary and secondary schools.

Clark, Gilbert; Enid Zimmerman; and Marilyn Zurmuehlen. *Understanding Art Testing: Past Influences, Norman C. Meier's Contributions, Present Concerns, and Future Possibilities.* Reston, Va.: National Art Education Association, 1987.

Discussion of testing children's art abilities and learning. Includes a review of past attempts at testing in art and an account of the testing research and efforts by Norman C. Meier in the mid-twentieth century.

Cohen, Elaine P., and Ruth S. Gainer. *Art: Another Language for Learning.* New York: Schocken Books, Inc., 1984.

For teachers who are not art specialists. Discusses aesthetic understanding. Use of situations experienced by authors to illustrate other objectives such as recognizing individuality, building self-confidence, and helping students to think.

Dunn, Phillip. *Promoting School Art: A Practical Approach.* Reston, Va.: National Art Education Association, 1987.

A handbook for anyone who needs practical ideas for making positive changes in the school art program. Includes a clearly stated rationale. Presents facts and figures to use when advocating for arts education.

Eisner, Elliot W. *Educating Artistic Vision.* New York: Macmillan Publishing Company, Inc., 1972.

A scholarly contemporary view on teaching art at all grade levels.

Fisher, Elaine Flory. *Aesthetic Awareness and the Child.* Itasca, Ill.: F. E. Peacock Publishers, Inc., 1978.

For the art specialist and classroom teacher. Deals with a multidisciplinary approach to art education, involving music, drama, poetry, dance, and other subjects such as science and social studies for kindergarten through grade seven. Goes beyond how-to-do-it projects and traditional aesthetics. Allows students to participate in a range of human expression and experience complex ideas in depth.

Janson, H.W., and Anthony F. Janson. *History of Art for Young People* (Third edition). New York: Harry N. Abrams, Inc., 1987.

Includes nearly 500 illustrations in color and black and white. An interpretive historical survey of painting, sculpture, architecture, and photography that cuts across Western civilization. Synoptic tables following each section and placing particular artworks within a broad context of religious and political history and technological and scientific advancements. Grades six through twelve.

Keightley, Moy. *Investigating Art: A Practical Guide for Young People.* Chicago: Facts on File, Inc., n.d.

Designed to help intermediate students to think visually and to be aware of visual ideas. Explores sensory properties with techniques, allowing children to make creative decisions.

Qualley, Charles. *Safety in the Artroom.* Worcester, Mass.: Davis Publications, Inc., 1986.

Easy-to-use guide providing information needed to ensure safety in the artroom. A resource for teachers, administrators, school business officers, and directors of instruction.

Smith, Ralph A. *Excellence in Art Education: Ideas and Initiatives.* Reston, Va.: National Art Education Association, 1987.

Responds to the excellence-in-education movement. Interprets excellence for purposes of developing art curriculum and instruction. Grades seven through twelve.

Uhlin, Donald H., and Edith De Chiara. *Art for Exceptional Children* (Third edition). Dubuque, Iowa: William C. Brown, Publishers, 1984.

Classic work on art for special children. Serves as a guide for teachers of children with special needs. Applicable to all levels of ability.

Wilson, Brent, and others. *Teaching Drawing from Art.* Worcester, Mass.: Davis Publications, Inc., 1987.

Presents a series of drawing ideas for all grades. Based on works of art that help students understand drawing as creative expression.

Interdisciplinary/Arts Selected References

Academic Preparation in the Arts. Academic Preparation Series. New York: The College Board, 1985.

Examines curricular ideas, teaching strategies, arts learning rationales, and related issues. Arts defined as separate fields of study which offer a distinctive contribution to preparation for college. Selected arts courses presented to illustrate how students might achieve the goals of production and performance skills, abilities in analysis and evaluation, and knowledge of the cultural contexts and historical development of the arts.

Bernardi, Bonnie, and others. *Partners in the Arts: An Arts in Education Handbook.* New York: American Council for the Arts, 1983.

A guide for schools on the use of community artists and arts institutions.

Endorsed by over 30 arts organizations. Thoroughly researched. Details how to build collaborations, raise money, and develop partnerships.

Broudy, Harry S. *The Role of Imagery in Learning.* Los Angeles: The Getty Center for Education in the Arts, 1987.

Presents the role of imagery in the learning of skills, concepts, attitudes, and values. Includes the theories and rationale needed to develop and justify arts programs as part of the core curriculum.

Coming to Our Senses: The Significance of the Arts for American Education. New York: American Council for the Arts, 1988.

Based on two years of research by a 25-member panel chaired by David Rockefeller, Jr. Presents 99 recommendations created by the panel to improve the condition of arts education throughout the nation.

Dudley, Louise, and others. *The Humanities* (Sixth edition). New York: McGraw-Hill Book Company, 1978.

A conceptual book covering all the arts. Examines the components (subject, form, function, organization, medium, and style) in music, dance, painting, sculpture, architecture, literature, and film.

Fowler, Charles. *Can We Rescue the Arts for America's Children? Coming to Our Senses 10 Years Later.* New York: American Council for the Arts, 1988.

Dissects what has happened to the arts in American schools in the past decade. Asks the reader to take part in the nationwide effort to produce a more accessible arts education. Wide-ranging issues addressed: educational reform in the arts, changing graduation requirements, the teaching of arts, art subjects which could and should be taught, who should be taught, and who should teach the arts.

Gardner, Howard. *Frames of Mind: The Theory of Multiple Intelligences.* New York: Basic Books, Inc., 1983.

Explores the multiple modes of thinking. Provides support for varied approaches and teaching methods, including teaching through the arts.

Humanities in America: A Report to the President, the Congress, and the American People. Washington, D.C.: National Endowment for the Humanities, 1988.

Reading, the Arts and the Creation of Meaning. Edited by Elliot W. Eisner. Reston, Va.: National Art Education Association, 1978.

Collection of essays exploring the relationship between art and a child's ability to read. First serious study of the relationship between reading text and reading visual images.

Technology in the Curriculum: Visual and Performing Arts. Sacramento: California State Department of Education, 1987.

A guide to using computers and instructional video in visual and performing arts instruction in kindergarten and grades one through twelve. Annotated compilation of quality ITV and software aligned with framework and curriculum standards. Sample lessons provided.

Toward a New Era in Arts Education: The Interlochen Symposium. New York: American Council for the Arts, 1988.

Report of a landmark conference of arts educators and representatives of major arts organizations in the United States who came to agreement on a direction for the arts in education.

Toward Civilization: A Report on Arts Education. Washington, D.C., National Endowment for the Arts.

Report on arts education in the United States. Identifies the arts that should be taught in school, presents the reasons for studying them, shows why the present state of arts education is unsatisfactory, and suggests avenues for the improvement of arts education.

Publications Available from the Department of Education

This publication is one of over 650 that are available from the California State Department of Education. Some of the more recent publications or those most widely used are the following:

ISBN	Title (Date of publication)	Price
0-8011-0271-5	Academic Honesty (1986)	$2.50
0-8011-0722-9	Accounting Procedures for Student Organizations (1988)	3.75
0-8011-0272-3	Administration of Maintenance and Operations in California School Districts (1986)	6.75
0-8011-0159-X	Arts for the Gifted and Talented, Grades 1—6 (1981)	2.75
0-8011-0216-2	Bilingual-Crosscultural Teacher Aides: A Resource Guide (1984)	3.50
0-8011-0238-3	Boating the Right Way (1985)	4.00
0-8011-0275-8	California Dropouts: A Status Report (1986)	2.50
0-8011-0783-0	California Private School Directory, 1988-89 (1988)	14.00
0-8011-0747-4	California Public School Directory (1989)	14.00
0-8011-0748-2	California School Accounting Manual (1988)	8.00
0-8011-0715-6	California Women: Activities Guide, K—12 (1988)	3.50
0-8011-0488-2	Caught in the Middle: Educational Reform for Young Adolescents in California Public Schools (1987)	5.00
0-8011-0760-1	Celebrating the National Reading Initiative (1989)	6.75
0-8011-0241-3	Computer Applications Planning (1985)	5.00
0-8011-0797-0	Desktop Publishing Guidelines (1989)	4.00
0-8011-0749-0	Educational Software Preview Guide, 1988-89 (1988)	2.00
0-8011-0796-2	Effective Language Arts Programs for Chapter I and Migrant Education (1989)	4.25
0-8011-0489-0	Effective Practices in Achieving Compensatory Education-Funded Schools II (1987)	5.00
0-8011-0041-0	English-Language Arts Framework for California Public Schools (1987)	3.00
0-8011-0731-8	English-Language Arts Model Curriculum Guide, K—8 (1988)	3.00
0-8011-0710-5	Family Life/Sex Education Guidelines (1987)	4.00
0-8011-0804-7	Foreign Language Framework for California Public Schools (1989)	5.50
0-8011-0289-8	Handbook for Physical Education (1986)	4.50
0-8011-0249-9	Handbook for Planning an Effective Foreign Language Program (1985)	3.50
0-8011-0320-7	Handbook for Planning an Effective Literature Program (1988)	3.00
0-8011-0179-4	Handbook for Planning an Effective Mathematics Program (1982)	2.00
0-8011-0290-1	Handbook for Planning an Effective Writing Program (1986)	2.50
0-8011-0224-3	Handbook for Teaching Cantonese-Speaking Students (1984)	4.50
0-8011-0680-X	Handbook for Teaching Japanese-Speaking Students (1987)	4.50
0-8011-0291-X	Handbook for Teaching Pilipino-Speaking Students (1986)	4.50
0-8011-0204-9	Handbook for Teaching Portuguese-Speaking Students (1983)	4.50
0-8011-0250-2	Handbook on California Education for Language Minority Parents—Chinese/English Edition (1985)	3.25*
0-8011-0737-7	Here They Come: Ready or Not—Report of the School Readiness Task Force (1988)	2.00
0-8011-0712-1	History–Social Science Framework for California Public Schools (1988)	6.00
0-8011-0782-2	Images: A Workbook for Enhancing Self-esteem and Promoting Career Preparation, Especially for Black Girls (1989)	6.00
0-8011-0227-8	Individual Learning Programs for Limited-English-Proficient Students (1984)	3.50
0-8011-0466-1	Instructional Patterns: Curriculum for Parenthood Education (1985)	12.00
0-8011-0208-1	Manual of First-Aid Practices for School Bus Drivers (1983)	1.75
0-8011-0209-X	Martin Luther King, Jr., 1929—1968 (1983)	3.25
0-8011-0358-4	Mathematics Framework for California Public Schools (1985)	3.00
0-8011-0664-8	Mathematics Model Curriculum Guide, K—8 (1987)	2.75
0-8011-0725-3	Model Curriculum for Human Rights and Genocide (1988)	3.25
0-8011-0252-9	Model Curriculum Standards: Grades 9—12 (1985)	5.50
0-8011-0762-8	Moral and Civic Education and Teaching About Religion (1988)	3.25
0-8011-0230-8	Nutrition Education—Choose Well, Be Well: A Resource Manual for Parent and Community Involvement in Nutrition Education Programs (1984)	4.50
0-8011-0185-9	Nutrition Education—Choose Well, Be Well: A Resource Manual for Preschool, Kindergarten, and Elementary Teachers (1982)	2.25
0-8011-0186-7	Nutrition Education—Choose Well, Be Well: A Resource Manual for Secondary Teachers (1982)	2.25
0-8011-0303-7	A Parent's Handbook on California Education (1986)	3.25
0-8011-0671-0	Practical Ideas for Teaching Writing as a Process (1987)	6.00
0-8011-0309-6	Program Guidelines for Hearing Impaired Individuals (1986)	6.00
0-8011-0258-8	Program Guidelines for Severely Orthopedically Impaired Individuals (1985)	6.00
0-8011-0684-2	Program Guidelines for Visually Impaired Individuals (1987)	6.00
0-8011-0213-8	Raising Expectations: Model Graduation Requirements (1983)	2.75
0-8011-0311-8	Recommended Readings in Literature, K—8 (1986)	2.25
0-8011-0745-8	Recommended Readings in Literature, K—8, Annotated Edition (1988)	4.50

*The following editions are also available, at the same price: Armenian/English, Cambodian/English, Hmong/English, Japanese/English, Korean/English, Laotian/English, Pilipino/English, Spanish/English, and Vietnamese/English.

0-8011-0214-6	School Attendance Improvement: A Blueprint for Action (1983)	2.75
0-8011-0189-1	Science Education for the 1980s (1982)	2.50
0-8011-0339-8	Science Framework for California Public Schools (1978)	3.00
0-8011-0354-1	Science Framework Addendum (1984)	3.00
0-8011-0665-6	Science Model Curriculum Guide, K—8 (1987)	3.25
0-8011-0668-0	Science Safety Handbook for California High Schools (1987)	8.75
0-8011-0738-5	Secondary Textbook Review: English (1988)	9.25
0-8011-0677-X	Secondary Textbook Review: General Mathematics (1987)	6.50
0-8011-0781-4	Selected Financial and Related Data for California Public Schools (1988)	3.00
0-8011-0265-0	Standards for Scoliosis Screening in California Public Schools (1985)	2.50
0-8011-0807-1	Statement on Competencies in Languages Other Than English Expected of Entering Freshmen: Phase I–French, German, Spanish (1988)	4.00
0-8011-0486-6	Statement on Preparation in Natural Science Expected of Entering Freshmen (1986)	2.50
0-8011-0318-5	Students' Rights and Responsibilities Handbook (1986)	2.75
0-8011-0234-0	Studies on Immersion Education: A Collection for U.S. Educators (1984)	5.00
0-8011-0682-6	Suicide Prevention Program for California Public Schools (1987)	8.00
0-8011-0739-3	Survey of Academic Skills, Grade 8: Rationale and Content for Science (1988)	2.50
0-8011-0192-1	Trash Monster Environmental Education Kit (for grade six)	23.00
0-8011-0236-7	University and College Opportunities Handbook (1984)	3.25
0-8011-0805-5	Visual and Performing Arts Framework for California Public Schools (1989 revision of 1982 edition)	6.00
0-8011-0237-5	Wet 'n' Safe: Water and Boating Safety, Grades 4—6 (1984)	2.50
0-8011-0194-8	Wizard of Waste Environmental Education Kit (for grade three)	20.00
0-8011-0670-2	Work Experience Education Instructional Guide (1987)	12.50
0-8011-0464-5	Work Permit Handbook for California Public Schools (1985)	6.00
0-8011-0686-9	Year-round Education: Year-round Opportunities—A Study of Year-round Education in California (1987)	5.00
0-8011-0270-7	Young and Old Together: A Resource Directory of Intergenerational Resources (1986)	3.00

Orders should be directed to:

California State Department of Education
P.O. Box 271
Sacramento, CA 95802-0271

Please include the International Standard Book Number (ISBN) for each title ordered.

Remittance or purchase order must accompany order. Purchase orders without checks are accepted only from governmental agencies. Sales tax should be added to all orders from California purchasers.

A complete list of publications available from the Department, including apprenticeship instructional materials, may be obtained by writing to the address listed above or by calling (916) 445-1260.

F88-541 (Second printing) 03-0347 300 6-89 15M